BLAZING THE WAY

Match Girls, Mill Girls and Other Fiery Females Whose Strikes Sparked a Revolution in Women's Rights

Elise Baker

© **Copyright 2023 - All rights reserved.**

The content contained within this book may not be reproduced, duplicated or transmitted without direct written permission from the author or the publisher.

Under no circumstances will any blame or legal responsibility be held against the publisher, or author, for any damages, reparation, or monetary loss due to the information contained within this book, either directly or indirectly.

Legal Notice:

This book is copyright protected. It is only for personal use. You cannot amend, distribute, sell, use, quote or paraphrase any part, or the content within this book, without the consent of the author or publisher.

Disclaimer Notice:

Please note the information contained within this document is for educational and entertainment purposes only. All effort has been executed to present accurate, up to date, reliable, complete information. No warranties of any kind are declared or implied. Readers acknowledge that the author is not engaged in the rendering of legal, financial, medical or professional advice. The content within this book has been derived from various sources. Please consult a licensed professional before attempting any techniques outlined in this book.

By reading this document, the reader agrees that under no circumstances is the author responsible for any losses, direct or indirect, that are incurred as a result of the use of the information contained within this document, including, but not limited to, errors, omissions, or inaccuracies.

TABLE OF CONTENTS

Introduction — VII

1. Harriet Hanson Robinson — 1
   Lowell Mill Girl
   - Early Life
   - From Bobbin Doffer to Bookworm
   - The Turn Out!
   - Harriet's Legacy

2. Sarah Bagley — 16
   Lowell Female Labor Reform Association President
   - Early Life
   - Fiery Feminist
   - Ten Hours, Ten Hours!
   - Sarah's Legacy

3. Sarah Chapman — 32

    Match Girls' Strike Committee Leader
        Early Life
        East Ender For Life
        The Bryant & May Match Factory Strike
        Sarah's Lasting Impact

4. Annie Besant   53
    Match Girls' Advocate, Journalist & Socialist
        Early Life
        Radical Feminism Takes Hold
        Annie Was The Link!
        Annie's Legacy

5. The Washing Amazons   69
    The Atlanta Washerwomen Strike
        What Led to the Strike?
        Washing Away Racial Oppression
        Consequences of the Strike
        The Collective Six

6. Lucy Parsons   86
    The Goddess of Anarchy
        Early Life
        Anarchy Takes Hold
        May Day!
        Lucy's Legacy

7. Clara Lemlich Shavelson   97
   An Incendiary Immigrant in New York
   Early Life
   A Firebrand in the Factory
   Uprising of the 20,000
   Clara's Legacy

8. Rose Schneiderman   108
   The Red Rose of Anarchy
   Early Life
   The Triangle Shirtwaist Factory Fire
   Bread and Roses
   Rose's Legacy

9. Conclusion   120

About the Author   126

Also By   128

References & Bibliography   130

INTRODUCTION

A strong woman is a woman determined to do something others are determined not be done.
—Marge Piercy

The Industrial Revolution was a time of great innovation, development, and progress across the globe, particularly in Europe, the U.S., and Britain. The Revolution forever changed the way the world manufactured, transported, and distributed products. Inventions such as the steam engine, electricity, and railway systems were adapted and used to build factories and vehicles and create machinery that transformed the means of production into the means of mass production. Industries like steel, chemicals, food, textiles, and transport grew exponentially, in a short period, because of the technological developments that were rapidly cropping up all over the modern Western world. The world also grew and became more interconnected on an economic level because the modernization of transport meant that goods could be transported in bulk within and between countries quickly. In this new industrial world, manufacturing became humanity's new form of agriculture: a means to survive.

The rural poor moved to cities that were hubs of industrial activity in the hope of finding employment to improve their lives and support their families. Capitalist entrepreneurs wanted to achieve the most by spending the least, resulting in the working class being subjected to dangerous working conditions, terrible living conditions, and few legal rights to assert against their abusive employers. Women and children were employed as factory workers as a source of cheap labor and paid less than men. Factory owners exploited these women and child workers, who often had no choice but to work to keep their households afloat.

History hasn't been kind to women; their stories have often been erased or retold incorrectly. Gender stereotyping and the oppression of women throughout history has left many important individuals silenced and many great stories untold. Our focus isn't on the famous male inventors of machinery and captains of industry, but on the groundbreaking achievements of just a few of the brave and strong women who blazed trails in their industries for female empowerment and workers' rights. They played a significant role in the history of labor relations and the industrialization of society. The female social activists portrayed in this book campaigned for their rights at work by assembling strikes, organizing trade unions, and distributing revolutionary information through the press that aided their causes. The events leading up to these strike actions, how they happened, and their impact will be examined.

We start in the textile mills of Lowell, Massachusetts, in the 1830s, where the majority of the factory workers were women, and introduce two fiery females who played a vital role in the Lowell Mill Strike. Harriet Hanson Robinson was a Lowell mill girl who became a prolific author, poet, and pioneer in the movement to grant women the right to vote. Sarah Bagley later took things up a notch by helping form the first-ever trade union to represent female workers.

The next duo of leading ladies challenged the prevailing Victorian norms during the Match Factory Strike of 1888 in the East End of London. Annie Besant, a social reformer and journalist, exposed the health conditions endured by women workers at the Bryant & May match factory. Sarah Chapman was the working class hero who led the strike committee, campaigned against the use of deadly chemicals in the manufacturing of matches, and established a trade union for the women workers at the factory.

The Atlanta Washerwomen Strike of 1881, led by the Washing Society, was made up mostly of African-American women who were emancipated slaves. The events of the strike were wrapped up in the deeply entrenched and systemic racism that marred the Southern States. The aftermath of the end of slavery in 1861 had a major impact on the labor market because of the mass urbanization of African-American families to the cities of America to look for work. The sour aftertaste of slavery still lingered in the city halls, and African-Americans had to contend with racism as they tried to survive and build generational wealth for the first time. This added an extra layer of cement to the brick wall the laundresses were trying to break through to set up their washing enterprises. The women fought for higher wages and the ability to control the laundry industry in Atlanta. The significance of this strike lies in the strength of the women involved, despite the oppression they experienced for being women of color. The "Atlanta Six" strike leaders knew the level of risk they were taking, and their bravery had a tremendous influence on labor activist and anarchist Lucy Parsons.

The final pair of female heroes is Clara Lemlich Shavelson and Rose Schneiderman. Clara, a 23-year-old Ukrainian immigrant working in the textile and garment industry, led an uprising of 20,000 female workers in the Triangle Shirtwaist Factory Strike of 1909 to protest against the working conditions. Tragically, all the warnings raised by the strikers were ignored, and the worst fears of the campaigners were realized two years later. In 1911, the sparks of catastrophe finally ignited, and the factory burned down, resulting in a great loss of life. After the fire, women's rights activist and trade unionist Rose Schneiderman campaigned for safer working conditions for women in the garment industry. Clara and Rose represent the millions of immigrants who left their home countries to escape persecution, only to land on American soil to be abused by the factory system.

The women presented here came from the most oppressed groups in society, yet they stood up to the most powerful groups by organizing collective and bold action in the form of strikes and protests. The outcomes of the strikes did not achieve all of their aims, but their success lies in their far-reaching impact on women's rights in the workplace and influence on the future attitudes of the female workforce.

In telling these stories, we must position the Industrial Revolution in the context of Victorian societal ideals of class, race, and gender. These ideals were heavily influenced by the Church of England, and this influence bled into how women were treated in the workplace. The Christian standard of femininity at the time was one of a passive, virtuous woman whom you would feel pity for because she was to act like a defenseless victim. Women who fell foul of the Victorian double standard of morality became "the fallen woman," and this social branding was a fate worse than death. The reality of working women was that they were a product of their environment and were often rough, rowdy, prone to brawling, and fond of cheap popular entertainment like music halls and variety shows. Victorian ideas of class were that the working classes were to be feared, seen as shiftless, and known for crime, alcoholism, and irresponsible behavior. The rhetoric of the upper classes was that the working class needed the firm hand of their "superiors" to keep them in place.

These stories of women's social activism, which span a century, present a rebalanced view of history in terms of the achievements of women in the era of the Industrial Revolution. Deep within each of these women, the match of rebellion was struck. From that point on, there was no turning back in their fight against discrimination.

Chapter One

Harriet Hanson Robinson

Lowell Mill Girl

It is too often a soulless organization; and its members forget that they are morally responsible for the souls and bodies, as well as for the wages, of those whose labor is the source of their wealth. – Harriet Hanson Robinson

The story of our first and youngest activist is set in the New England town of Lowell, Massachusetts, sometimes referred to as the "Cradle of the American Industrial Revolution" (Dublin, 1979). It became a hub of industrial activity during the 1800s when successful factory owner, Francis Cabot Lowell, established the Waltham-Lowell factory system that changed the textile industry forever. The system created a streamlined production line that was the first of its kind in the U.S. The factory aimed to process raw cotton into cloth for use in textiles. The cotton was spun, weaved, dyed, and cut in the factories. This revolutionary system caused Lowell to become known as "The City of Spindles" during this era of industrialization in the U.S.

Francis Cabot Lowell had toured the "dark Satanic mills of Britain" (as described by William Blake in his poem *And Did Those Feet In Ancient Time*) and had a vision of a clean, wholesome workforce of country girls who could be intellectually stimulated by discussion groups and protected by older women who ran the boarding houses. The workers became known colloquially as the Belles of New England, illustrating the idealized view of female factory workers at that time.

Lowell's textile mills relied on human labor to keep their spindles spinning. The workforce in the Lowell mills was initially a mix of men, women, and children. However, by the 1830s, women made up about 75% of the employees in the mills, with most of them aged between 15 and 30. A workforce of New England farm girls was drafted in from the rural countryside. In the early years, the Lowell mill had a literacy and education program with evening classes offered for the mill workers. Many young girls were enticed to work at the mill with the exciting promise of earning their own cash wages and independence from fathers and husbands.

Harriet Hanson Robinson started working in the mills when she was only 11-years-old. Even at this young age,

Harriet had a fire in her heart for standing up for what was right for the female workforce she was part of. Harriet's story represents how the Lowell mill girls collectively found their unique and controversial voice through the written word during a dark time of oppression disguised as opportunity.

Early Life

Like most New England mill girls, Harriet's ancestors were originally from England, and they traveled to America as English settlers. Harriet was born in Boston, Massachusetts, in 1825, just as industrialization was tightening its steely grip on the east coast of America. The only girl in the family, she had three brothers, one older and two younger Harriet's father, a carpenter, died when she was only five-years-old, leaving her mother, also named Harriet, a young widow with no means to provide for her family.

America had recently gained independence from the British in 1776, and it should have been a time of hope, but life in Boston wasn't easy for the Hansons. The young family lived in poverty as Harriet's mother tried to make a living by running a convenience store. Even though they were poor and women were discouraged from expressing their thoughts and opinions, Harriet, like most mill girls, could read and write from a young age. Despite the financial hardship, Harriet's mother refused to split their family apart. It was common for children to leave the household and look for work before they even reached the age of 12. However, the Hansons, as a complete family unit, packed up and moved to the town of Lowell in the hopes of increasing their earning power while staying together as a family.

Moving to Lowell would change Harriet's life forever. The Hansons didn't realize this, but they had stepped into the hub of the industrialization of the textile industry in America. Francis Cabot Lowell pumped money into the town to turn it into a shining beacon of success in the cotton milling sector. The powers that be wanted Lowell to be a flagship milling town to showcase Mr. Lowell's Waltham-Lowell production and labor system of manufacturing. The town operated on a system of organized labor where young women between the ages of 15 and 35 were recruited to work in the mills. The factory owners then invested in building hostels or boarding houses where the women workers lived, and Harriet's mother became a manager of one of them to support her family. The houses became hubs of social activity for the women working in the mills. The discussions and attitudes that began to simmer at boarding houses, like the one run by Harriet's mother, were instrumental in bringing about the revolutionary events of the Lowell Mill Strike, and we'll explore how a bit later on.

Harriet started her first part-time job as a bobbin doffer in the Tremont Mill when she was just 11-years-old, and her earnings of $2 per week contributed to running the family home. Many children were employed at the mills because child labor was acceptable in early industrial America. Children were useful because their small hands made winding the cotton back onto the whirring bobbins easier. Harriet was tasked with replacing the bobbins of cotton used up during the weaving process. This only took 15 minutes at a time, but it was dangerous work; accidents and injuries, such as losing a finger, were common. The factory owners allowed the children to play during their breaks from replacing bobbins, but the heat and noise of the machines were deafening. Harriet's young start as a Lowell mill girl later motivated her to pick up her torch in protest with other mill girls and light the path for many women after her.

From Bobbin Doffer to Bookworm

The combination of Harriet's respect for education, her voracious appetite for knowledge, and her observations of life at the Lowell mills were like pouring gasoline on the fire of the women's labor movements at Lowell. She was educated even before she became a bobbin doffer at the Lowell mills. From her later writings about the Lowell mill strikes and historical accounts, it appears that Harriet saw education as both a means of survival as a mill girl and a source of comfort and distraction from the harsh conditions of factory work.

The town of Lowell already had a reputation as a somewhat sophisticated place of opportunity in terms of culture, education, religion, and exposure to this new world of industry. Many of the young women who responded to Francis Cabot Lowell's call for workers came to Lowell to broaden their educational horizons while earning a fair wage in the factories. Harriet's mother might have been similarly motivated to move her family to Lowell because of the possible opportunities for young Harriet.

At age 15, Harriet took a two-year break to study. Her studies included how to compose written work and the rules of grammar, as well as Latin and French. She endeavored to open her mind beyond the confines of the factory walls by learning concepts and schools of thought that were way beyond her years or social class.

When Harriet returned to work at the mills at the age of 17, she was known amongst her colleagues as always having a book in her hands in her spare time. While she worked in the mill, she was an active book club, writing group, and literary group member. Harriet's role and influence in those female communities helped to shape and embolden them. She took full advantage of the cultural epicenter and exchange of ideas that Lowell was known for. *The Lowell Offering* was a monthly magazine that featured poems, short stories, and fiction pieces written by the Lowell mill girls. Harriet was a notable contributor to the publication and became known for her thought-provoking poems containing outright or implied references to the harsh realities of working in the mills.

Harriet used her intellect and forward-thinking mindset to carefully observe her surroundings. She knew her colleagues were trying to gain independence, even though the odds were stacked against them as women and workers. Even at the young age of 11, before she had gained much life experience, Harriet joined the other mill girls in the strike without a second thought because she knew their working conditions were unjust. Her involvement in the strike might have also been motivated by the deep sense of community, family, and unity that her mother had instilled in her and her brothers after losing their father. Harriet's mother taught her from a young age that some things are worth fighting for just because they are right.

Harriet's written observations of life in Lowell provided a rare inside view of what being a mill girl was really like, including the exciting cultural exchange among the female workforce, the unique social activities through the boarding house communities, and the harsh realities of the backbreaking work in the textile factories.

The Turn Out!

What attracted many of the mill girls to Lowell was the search for financial independence and a taste of freedom. "The thought that I am living on no one is a happy one, indeed," one young woman wrote (The Attic, n.d.). The initial excitement faded after they arrived and started working in the textile factories. Their living conditions were far from fancy. The many boarding houses, like the one Harriet's mother managed, housed between 25 and 40 women and girls in three-story high buildings with about 10 rooms in each one. Living quarters were cramped, and privacy was non-existent.

The older women who ran the boarding houses were in charge of cooking, cleaning, and making sure female workers acted in a morally correct way, including ensuring church attendance on their one free day. The Waltham-Lowell system was closely tied to the ethics and principles of the church, so the women were not allowed to deviate from the oppressive religious standards. Rent at a boarding house cost about $1 a week, and the average female factory worker in Lowell earned about $4 a week. However, the mill girls developed close bonds with each other in their cramped living arrangements. Harriet wrote about the way new girls were welcomed in the boarding house by more senior house members. They had their own unique culture and sense of camaraderie, and they helped the new recruits adjust to city life.

The working conditions at the Lowell mills were tough. Women workers were paid about half of what men earned, so their worth was already demeaned as they entered the workforce. The mill girls worked a grueling 75 hours a week, on average. They started work before the sun rose and ended their 10-hour shifts once it had set again, so they saw very little daylight. Besides the unfair payment scale and long hours, the work itself was dangerous. The women were packed into rooms with little ventilation for long hours and made to do repetitive work. The rooms often overheated because of the heavy steam machinery being operated within them. The air quality was poor because of the cotton particles, dyes, and textile dust in the atmosphere. This left the women susceptible to lung conditions that made it difficult to breathe. They were supervised by strict foremen who had the right to discipline the women and make sure they complied with factory rules. A song the young girls sang depicting the harsh working conditions had the following poignant lyrics:

> "Oh! Isn't it a pity, such a pretty girl as I
> Should be sent to the factory
> To pine away and die?
> Oh! I cannot be a slave
> I will not be a slave
> For I'm so fond of liberty
> That I cannot be a slave."
> (Hanson Robinson, 1898).

The first strike or "turn-out" as the mill girls called it, took place in 1834 after factory owners announced that they would cut wages by 15%. Groups of women within the boarding houses, known as "operatives," organized meetings and decided to strike in protest of the wage decrease. The strike was unsuccessful, and most of the women went back to work for less pay, however, the unity shared by the mill girls in the 1834 strike served as flint or drywood to ignite the strike of 1836.

In 1836, the Lowell factory owners decided to raise the price of rent at the boarding houses without a proportional rise in the women's wages. The mill girls banded together once again and organized a strike to protest the increased rent charges, forming the Factory Girls' Association for strength and unity.

Despite Harriet's desire to improve their lives, her mother lost her job as a boarding house supervisor for the Tremont Mills as an act of revenge for her young daughter "turning out" on strike. Harriet was caught between protecting her family and solidarity with the mill workers. For the first time in American history, women were standing up for themselves as workers, and Harriet wanted to be a part of making history.

> "The agent of the corporation where I then worked took some small revenges on the supposed ringleaders; on the principle of sending the weaker to the wall, my mother was turned away from her boarding-house, that functionary saying, 'Mrs. Hanson, you could not prevent the older girls from turning out, but your daughter is a child, and her you could control'" (Robinson, 1898).

About 1,500 women workers walked out of the Lowell mills during the strike of 1836. It was one of the first strikes for the rights of the female workforce and better working conditions in factories in America. The first recorded strike for workers' rights during the Industrial Revolution in America occurred in Pawtucket in 1824. The entire Pawtucket community felt the looming sense of destruction that the first cotton mill was threatening. They saw how the wealthy sought to control the working class by depriving them of fair wages. The environmental impact of the factory also played a role in the strike, as many of the area's natural resources, like rivers, were destroyed by the factory runoff. The Pawtucket strike was led by about 100 female workers, and the strikers set the mill alight on the final day. The Lowell mill girls followed in the fiery footsteps of their passionate predecessors. Harriet recorded a few of her experiences of the economic oppression happening at Lowell in her book, *Loom and Spindle*, as follows:

> When it was announced that the wages were to be cut down, great indignation was felt, and it was decided to strike, en masse. This was done. The mills were shut down, and the girls went in procession from their several corporations to the "grove" on Chapel Hill, and listened to "incendiary" speeches from early labor reformers. One of the girls stood on a pump, and gave vent to the feelings of her companions in a neat speech, declaring that it was their duty to resist all attempts at cutting down the wages. This was the first time a woman had spoken in public in Low-

ell (Hanson Robinson, 1898).

The 1836 strike in Lowell met with limited success. The boarding house rents were not raised, but neither were wages. Perhaps its success lay in striking fear into the hearts of the factory owners by hinting at the workers' collective power to protest against oppressive and abusive systems. They had always expected women workers to "know their place" and remain silent while being the backbone of the textile industry. Harriet contributed to the strike by later recording her experiences of that time in vivid written accounts in books and poems. Her writings became a narrative for female factory workers across America during the Industrial Revolution. Harriet wisely observed that the new labor system was a form of modernized slavery and threatened to destroy the morale of the workers who were treated like the machines they were trained to operate. Harriet described the events of the strike in her own words in her book, *Loom and Spindle*, as follows:

> My own recollection of this first strike (or "turn out" as it was called) is very vivid. I worked in a lower room, where I had heard the proposed strike fully, if not vehemently, discussed; I had been an ardent listener to what was said against this attempt at "oppression" on the part of the corporation, and naturally I took sides with the strikers. When

the day came on which the girls were to turn out, those in the upper rooms started first, and so many of them left that our mill was at once shut down. Then, when the girls in my room stood irresolute, uncertain what to do, asking each other, "Would you? " or "Shall we turn out?" and not one of them having the courage to lead off, I, who began to think they would not go out, after all their talk, became impatient, and started on ahead, saying, with childish bravado, "I don't care what you do, I am going to turn out, whether anyone else does or not;" and I marched out, and was followed by the others (Robinson, 1898).

Harriet's Legacy

After the 1836 strike, Harriet went back to working in the mills. In a cruel twist, her family was worse off than before due to her mother losing her job as a boarding house manager when Harriet was named as a participant in the strike. She used her time at the mills after 1836 to further mobilize female operatives through her writing. Harriet wielded her pen like a sword against the oppression of women, and her published work became the voice of the under-represented mill girls. Harriet wrote pieces for the most controversial publications of the time, called *The Lowell Offering* and *The Voice of Industry*, that challenged the status quo in Lowell in terms of women's rights and workers' rights.

Harriet went on to become a journalist after she married fellow writer William Stevens Robinson. After raising a family and taking on administrative jobs, Harriet joined the Women's Suffrage Organization in Massachusetts, where she tirelessly campaigned for women's rights, especially the right to vote. Harriet toured her state, giving speeches, having meetings with local governments, and networking with other suffrage activists of the time. In her book *Loom and Spindle*, she recalls the influence of the strike on her later life as a social activist as follows:

> As I looked back at the long line that followed me, I was more proud than I have ever been since at any success I may have achieved, and more proud than I shall ever be again until my own beloved State gives to its women citizens the right of suffrage (Robinson, 1898).

She encouraged her daughters to also break the mold and take on jobs that were usually occupied by men. When Harriet's husband died, she threw herself back into writing, and this is when her written accounts of her days in the Lowell mills became part of the narrative of working women across America. She wrote *Loom and Spindle* in 1898. It tells a vivid story of the Lowell mills, the strikes, her own struggles, and of daily life in newly industrialized America. In her own quietly powerful and logical way, until her death in 1911, Harriet advocated for the equal treatment of women in all spheres of life. American women were granted the right to vote in 1919. The embers of Harriet's legacy continued to burn long after she left the Lowell mills and put down her pen. If Harriet gave the mill girls their voice, our next inflammable icon, Sarah Bagley, gave them their legs.

Chapter Two

SARAH BAGLEY

Lowell Female Labor Reform Association President

When our rights are trampled upon and we appeal in vain to our legislators, what are we to do? Shall not our voice be heard? – Sarah Bagley

The desire for change and justice was lit within the female community at Lowell by the 1836 strike. The textile industry in industrial America began to boom as the successful systems and machinery developed in Lowell spread further afield. More small milling towns popped up and attracted workers from far and wide. As mentioned in Harriet's story, the promise of a better life with some education and independence and a chance to earn cash wages of their own brought many young women into these milling towns to look for work. In fact, the number of workers in Lowell grew from 6,100 workers and 17,000 residents in 1836 to a staggering 11,400 workers and 33,000 residents by 1850 (Dublin, 1975). These new workers were still mostly women but now included Irish immigrants, who began to move into Lowell and occupy jobs at the new and existing mills throughout the 1840s. Industrial progress in Lowell was rapid, but all it did was widen the gap between the wealthy elite and the downtrodden working class.

The changes and expansion of the mills in Lowell served the rich men who owned the factories, while the lives of the women who worked in them became more cramped, costly, and intellectually stifling. The determined groups of female operatives were now more closely bonded than ever, thanks to the impact of the iconic 1836 Lowell Mill Strike, the cinders of which still fueled the drive for improved working conditions. These women, often the breadwinners for their families, were the workforce that drove the success of the textile mills. However, their contributions and rights as women employees were neither acknowledged nor respected.

Early Life

Sarah was born in Candia, New Hampshire, in 1806, one of four children in a family from a large group of English settlers who had carved a life for themselves in the small railroad town of Candia. It was difficult to avoid hearing about or being exposed to the news of industrialization in other parts of the country because the railway lines that transported workers, goods, and supplies to factories down south to Massachusetts ran through the close-knit community of Candia. It would have caused some upheaval within the small town and piqued the interest of its inhabitants, including Sarah.

Those living in rural New England were encouraged to see factory work as a step up from their sometimes abject poverty. The entire country was on the brink of a new era, and citizens living in the rural areas were probably both curious and afraid of the industries storming through their small towns. Sarah might have seen the new mills as an opportunity for social and economic advancement.

Sarah left her home in Candia at 31 to join the workforce in Lowell in 1837 as a more mature mill worker. She would have been familiar with the stories about the controversial strikes or "turn-outs" of 1834 and 1836 led by female workers whose labor disruptions were publicized as failures by the biased media of the time. The women activists were portrayed as uncouth vigilantes, intent on disrupting the peaceful and contented lives of the other factory workers who were demurely grateful for their jobs.

Sarah started as a weaver in the Hamilton Mills. She tasted a bit of the financial independence she was promised when she came to Lowell in 1840 by buying her family home and being able to support her family back in Candia. The fact that she was older than most of the other young women working at the mills gave her a more realistic insight into the life of a female factory worker. There were no rose-tinted glasses for Sarah.

Fiery Feminist

Sarah was part of the first generation of young women who became working women, coming to Lowell looking for opportunities, education, self-discovery, and new beginnings. One of the notable strikes occurred when Sarah started in the mills involving about 70 female workers employed at the Middlesex Mills putting down their tools after they were expected to operate and manage two looms simultaneously. Looms were large machines used to weave threads of fabric together tightly and concisely. It was difficult work, and their wages didn't increase even though more work was required. This was a common trend throughout the mills in Lowell. The industry was expanding, but the factory owners were hoarding their wealth instead of treating workers fairly.

Being a mill girl meant inevitably staying in one of the many boarding houses owned by or leased to the factory owners. These boarding houses had their own culture, and there was an unspoken thread of comradeship among the mill girls. Their resistance to the oppressive capitalist regime was openly discussed at these hostels; it was a rite of passage to be exposed to women's groups, literary groups, book clubs, and political meetings if you were a new mill girl. Sarah soon became an integral part of this cultural hub of intellectual thought and political discussion because, like Harriet, Sarah stood up for what was right on instinct, without a second thought about the consequences. She was also an intellectual giant and immediately began to see the cracks in the factory system as soon as she joined. She was wise enough to see both the benefits and downsides of being a female factory worker. Sarah noted this in one of her contributions to *The Lowell Offering*, where she wrote about the "Pleasures of Factory Life." It was a tongue-in-cheek social and economic commentary where she acknowledged the perceived sense of freedom given to her by earning a salary and being a working woman. In the same piece, Sarah controversially noted that the pleasures of factory life, "were like angels' visits: few and far between" (Wright, 1979). One of the pleasures she did note in her article was the pleasure of freedom of thought:

> As the body goes through the motions of twisting, pulling, and plucking, all the powers of the mind are made active. Who can closely examine all the movements of the complicated, curious machinery, and not be led to the reflection that the mind is boundless and that it can accomplish almost anything on which it fixes its attention! (Giaimo, 2017).

Her philosophical views on how the factory system broke women down only deepened the more time she spent as a mill girl. Sarah believed women needed a social and political identity because they contributed to society and the economy. To Sarah, this meant that the female workforce should have their inherent rights acknowledged. Many women who were mill girls had no social or political identity at home on the farms they grew up on because their fathers made every decision for them. Women also had no rights in marriage because the husband controlled everything and made decisions on behalf of the couple. The work they'd have to do at home was equally laborious and difficult as factory work. Most farming families were self-sufficient, meaning that the women made everything they used from scratch, including clothes, soap, butter, candles, furniture, and cheese. Their chores and hobbies bled into one; this became the life of a young woman living in rural America. There was no opportunity to even dream about a different life until the metaphorical dust from the textile mills found its way under the doors of their rural homes and attracted their daughters to move into the city. Many women came to Lowell to escape these religious, social, and political restrictions. They were like refugees as they came to Lowell in droves. Just like a refugee, running away to escape oppression doesn't mean you forfeit your human rights and dignity.

Sarah felt that, as a factory worker, there were inherent rights that women were entitled to just by virtue of their work. She highlighted that being in such an innovative environment like Lowell meant that the mill girls had to think beyond the horizons and societal lines they were told never to cross. The working class rising up and taking ownership of the means of production was a controversial topic developed and discussed by German philosopher Karl Marx. He was writing his *Communist Manifesto* at the same time as the Industrial Revolution was leaving its toxic cloud of smoke over workers, whose choices for survival were dwindling as capitalism ran rampant across the West like an unstoppable steam-powered machine. The mill girls in Lowell were beginning to catch wind of these revolutionary new ideas about workers' rights, and Sarah's opinions helped to trigger them into further action after 1836.

Sarah was deeply religious and a romantic at heart. Through her writings, she tried to highlight the softer and more feminine side of the mill girls. They weren't the hardened factory workers who were constantly covered in soot and grease that the press portrayed them to be after the 1836 strike. The girls were in the habit of writing poetry and pinning their verses to the looms they worked on. Their femininity was shown in the way they would place flowers in the dingy weaving rooms. Their thirst for knowledge was evident in the math problems and equations stuck to the factory walls. They were still women and deserved the freedom and time to be just that.

Sarah wrote of her desire for women workers to be able to appreciate flowers, nature, and the finer things in life, outside of their lives as factory workers. She used her writing to paint vivid pictures of the lives the mill girls could have and asked them to remember the lives they left behind. She saw nature as a physical representation of God on earth, and she felt that the work in the factories was disconnecting them from nature. She was way ahead of her time in her thinking because she emphasized how the building of factories separated people from nature and God's natural creations. Her concerns for the environment were progressive for the time. Sarah's romantic sentiments and forward-thinking ideas about women at work and the consequences of industrialization would form the arrowhead of her focused career as an activist in Lowell and beyond.

Ten Hours, Ten Hours!

The labor "rules" laid down by factory owners in Lowell were created to serve their own purposes and to make the exploitation of factory workers legally and socially acceptable. There was barely any distinction between church and state, and mills ran according to accepted religious principles, including the expectation that all workers must observe Christian holy days. The factory owners used the rapid economic growth of the textile industry in Lowell and the supposed benefits their businesses brought to the region to justify how they mistreated their workers. What they failed to consider is that most of the female workforce at Lowell had their roots laid in the land. They were primarily farmers' daughters from rural areas, and they knew they weren't being treated humanely. Because of women like Sarah, the women of Lowell were never likely to comply with the false promises of a better life touted by the entrepreneurs who owned the means of production.

By the 1840s, the mill girls' working hours had increased, the work got more difficult and dangerous, and their living conditions had become even more cramped. Wages were never increased, only decreased, and employee rights were non-existent. The meetings of the female operatives who organized strikes dwindled to rare occasions, because many women had moved out of the boarding houses and into private housing. The women were seeking hope and leadership as they trudged along in the factories. Before we progress through Sarah's involvement in Lowell, let's examine the impact of two other mill girls who are less well-known but who also stoked the fire of revolution at Lowell.

Harriet Farley was a mill girl who also came to Lowell from New Hampshire. She was a talented writer and became the editor of *The Lowell Offering*, the iconic publication written by and for the mill girls. Farley joined the abolitionist movement to abolish slavery in the U.S. She used her reputation as an anti-slavery feminist to draw subtle and strategic parallels between slavery and the lives of the mill girls in the textile factories. She wrote that women's independence and freedom to be treated as equal was diminished by the oppressive nature of the factory system. Farley stated that the mill girls were better off living their rural lives than subjecting themselves to the abuse of mill owners, but they had to fight for something because they couldn't return to lives where they had little to no control. Farley's works for *The Lowell Offering* were noticed by famous author Charles Dickens, and she contributed to the narrative of mill girls that continues to inspire women today.

Originally from Vermont, mill girl Mary Paul came to Lowell in 1845. She wrote a series of letters to her father between 1845 and 1862 that display the transformation of her mindset about factory life in Lowell. She starts out hopeful and optimistic about moving to Lowell, viewing factory work as an opportunity for independence and achievement. Mary goes on to describe a few of the many accidents that often happened at the mills, some of which were fatal. Her letters report how difficult life was in the factories and how hard the women had to work to make a living. Mary's letters in 1846 characterize the extreme working conditions and the struggle the mill girls endured as the cost of living crept up but they were constantly threatened with their wages being dropped if they didn't work until they were exhausted. "It is *very* hard indeed and sometimes I think I shall not be able to endure it. I never worked so hard in my life but perhaps I shall get used to it" (University of Albany, n.d.).

Sarah Bagley worked in Lowell at the same time as Harriet and Mary, and they experienced similar hardships. Sarah could no longer stand back and work in silence as a compliant factory worker. She became an even more radical labor activist due to her growing frustration. She and five other female operatives got together in 1844 to form the first-ever trade union to represent female workers, the Lowell Female Labor Reform Association (LFLRA). This bold display of activism resulted in Sarah's dismissal from her job at the mill, but the spark of resistance had already been lit within her, and she refused to back down. She defiantly broadened the reach of the LFLRA by joining forces with the New England Workingmen's Association and brought the organization's membership up to 600 members.

Sarah was elected president of the LFLRA, a post she held for three years. Sarah used her influential position to speak up in public against the owners of the Lowell mills and how they treated their workers. Her main areas of focus were trying to reduce the working hours for the mill girls to 10 hours and to improve health conditions within the factories. To reach even more supporters, *The Voice of Industry* was created. It was a publication that Sarah managed and contributed to that highlighted social and political issues that impacted the women of Lowell. In 1845, Sarah petitioned the Massachusetts legislature to improve the women's working conditions and quality of life:

> We the undersigned peaceable, industrious and hardworking men and women of Lowell, in view of our condition—the evils already come upon us, by toiling from 13 to 14

hours per day, confined in unhealthy apartments, exposed to the poisonous contagion of air, vegetable, animal and mineral properties, debarred from proper Physical Exercise, Mental discipline, and Mastication cruelly limited, and thereby hastening us on through pain, disease and privation, down to a premature grave, pray the legislature to institute a ten-hour working day in all of the factories of the state. —Signed, John Quincy Adams Thayer, Sarah G. Bagley, James Carle and 2,000 others mostly women (*The Voice of Industry*, 1845).

Sarah's role in the revolutionary Ten-Hour Movement left permanent scorch marks on the textile mill industry. In 1845, Sarah and the LFLRA protested the 12 to 14-hour work days the women had to work in the factories. They demanded that it be reduced to 10 hours. "Is anyone such a fool as to suppose that out of six thousand factory girls in Lowell, sixty would be there if they could help it?" (The Attic, n.d.). The group started a petition for the Ten-Hour Movement, and through Sarah's public campaigning, they managed to get over 2000 signatures, most of which came from female workers. In her speeches and writings to create awareness about the movement, Sarah drew powerful parallels by highlighting that prisoners worked fewer hours than the mill girls did. "Let no one suppose the 'factory girls' are without guardians. We are placed in the care of overseers who feel under moral obligation to look after our interests" (National Park Service, 2021). She explained that their intellectual development was stifled by being cooped up in the dusty and dreary factories for 14 hours a day.

The Massachusetts legislature offered the LFLRA an opportunity to speak in court on behalf of the Ten-Hour Movement. Women publicly speaking against the dominant male authority was unheard of. Sarah was undeterred by how she was expected to behave. Sarah once again defied gender stereotypes and spoke up in court on behalf of the Ten-Hour Movement with her five LFLRA associates. The women described their working conditions, their illnesses from being overworked, and how decreasing their working hours would benefit them and their community. The legislature rejected the proposal and chose to reduce working hours by only 30 minutes. However, news of the LFLRA standing up to the oppressive authorities spread to neighboring New England states, which reduced the working day of factory workers to 10 hours. Massachusetts would only adopt the 10-hour work day much later in 1874. The strike and petition achieved its aims of shortening the working day for mill girls across New England.

Sarah's Legacy

Sarah was one of the many mill workers who went on to be active in the suffragist and abolitionist movements. She fought for women's rights in all spheres of life and publicly denounced slavery throughout the rest of her life. After the technology arrived in Massachusetts, she became the first female telegraph operator in the U.S. Sarah quit after a year after she realized there was a pay gap between her and her male co-workers that performed the same job she did. Once again, Sarah was ahead of her time in recognizing the discrimination involved in the gender pay gap that still exists today. A famous quote from Sarah highlights this recognition:

> "I am sick at heart when I look into the social world and see women so willingly made a dupe to the beastly selfishness of man" (National Park Service, 2021).

After pioneering for women in the telecommunications industry, Sarah went back to Lowell in 1848. She went back to work in the Hamilton mills but continued to resist and campaign for further reform and women's rights, especially the right to vote in the New England area. Sarah's work for women's rights wasn't limited to female factory workers. She joined forces with the religious sect of conservative settlers in America known as Quakers to help shelter abused women and prostitutes at the Rosine Home in Philadelphia in 1849.

Sarah was married in 1851 and moved to New York to become a homeopathic doctor, where she and her husband opened their own homeopathic practice. Her decision to take up homeopathy harks back to Sarah's deep connection to nature and her emphasis on appreciating its presence and importance in her early writings as a mill girl. Their practice eventually led them to start manufacturing homeopathic remedies that included herbal medicines. Sarah died in Philadelphia in 1889, but her legacy lives on in the feminist movements, protests, and petitions that still occur today. The plight and bravery of the mill girls have entered the popular imagination and cultural life through novels, dramatizations, and even a recent musical called *Mill Girls*. The musical was written "for the millions of girls who are too bright, too badass, too interesting, and still pushed to the margins" (Mill Girls Musical, n.d.). The organizers behind the musical have used their platform to collect signatures that they intend to display at the Lowell National Historical Park in commemoration of the lengths these women went to for change and to pave the way toward gender equality.

We'll be revisiting the conditions of American textile workers in the early 1900s in later chapters that explore the Triangle Shirtwaist Factory Strike. The Industrial Revolution was in full swing in Britain too. Before returning to the U.S., let's hop across the pond through the haze of smog that hung in the air as factories sprang up in England. The strong connection between the labor movements in the second half of the 1800s and the abolition movements to abolish slavery is clearly seen in incidents such as the Cotton Mill Famine that occurred in Lancashire in the north of England in the early 1860s. Most of the textile industry's supply of raw cotton was farmed and harvested by African-American slaves in the southern states of the U.S. The breakout of the American Civil War in 1861 saw the southern states use their cotton supply as leverage for military support from the British. England's cotton supply from the U.S. was abruptly cut off when ships full of cotton intended to be exported to Liverpool, England, were prevented from making the journey. Just like Lowell, many small towns in England were built around the mills and needed the work provided by the textile industry to survive. With no cotton to process, Lancashire mills went bankrupt and began to shut down. The mostly female workforce from the factories lost their jobs, leaving their families to starve with no steady income. After a year of suffering, starvation, and panic, Lancashire mill workers wrote a letter to U.S. President Abraham Lincoln, asking him for help. Lincoln sent over relief in the form of bags of flour and other food. This period was one that saw England and the U.S. unite for the greater good, even though blood was being shed on American soil in the Civil War. A monument honoring Abraham Lincoln for his efforts to help the mill workers during the Cotton Mill Famine was erected in Manchester in 1986. In keeping with the theme of transatlantic parallels, our next stop takes us to London in the late 1800s, where we'll meet two fiery females who spearheaded the memorable Bryant & May Match Factory Strike.

Chapter Three

SARAH CHAPMAN

Match Girls' Strike Committee Leader

Don't hold back because you think it's unladylike. We shouldn't be shamed out of our anger. We should be using it. —Jessica Valenti

London in the late 1800s was a place of stark contrasts. The divide between the wealthy elite and the hard-working yet devastatingly poor working class was harsh and disturbingly vivid. Industrialization had swept through most of England by the second half of the century, and factories became the central features around English towns. Urbanization had occurred in previous decades on a mass scale, where workers left their homes in the country and traveled to the city to look for work in various industries. London was often cloaked by a thick smog hovering over its overcrowded, dirty streets. Disease and poverty were the norm, and factory workers were packed into every available lodging to try and work to support their families. The works of prolific author Charles Dickens depicted the conditions of the abject poverty of London's working class. His novels, such as *Oliver Twist* and the popular story, *A Christmas Carol*, provide a critical social commentary of life in 19th century England, where your class determined your fate and lot in life.

The pair of revolutionary women you'll learn about over the next two chapters worked in London's East End in the 1880s in the Bryant and May match factory. They were known as "match girls" but had little in common with the titular character in the Hans Christian Anderson tale *The Little Match Girl*, published in 1845. Unlike the child in this tale, which appealed to the Victorian image of "the good victim" who suffered quietly, full of pathos, the real match girls were often loud and boisterous. In her 2011 book *Striking A Light*, author and historian Louise Raw paints a colorful picture of match workers who worked hard and played hard. They were fond of frequenting music halls and gin palaces and were not above brawling in public. Local politician, George Duckworth noted the following in 1897:

> Bryant and May have a rough set of girls. There are 2000 of them when they are busy. Rough and rowdy, but not bad morally. They fight with their fists to settle their differences, not in the factory for that is forbid-

> den, but in the streets when they leave work in the evening. A ring is formed, they fight like men and are not interfered with by the police (Matchgirls' Memorial, n.d.).

The match women had a great sense of team spirit, forming the "Feathers Club" to pool resources for buying extravagant hats to share on nights out. Notable lawyer and magistrate of the time, Montagu Williams, observed the match women's recreational activities and fashion sense in his book called *Round London, Down East and Up West*, 1892:

> "...to have half-a-dozen of these girls marching down the Bow Road singing at the top of their voices the chorus of 'Ta-ra-ra Boom-de-ay,' or 'Knocked 'em in the Old Kent Road' ... is a little irritating to quiet-loving citizens" (Williams, 1892). "They have fashions of their own; they delight in a quantity of colour; and they can no more live without their large hats and huge feathers than 'Arry can live without his bell-bottom trousers" (Williams, 1892).

Local economist Clara Collet also highlighted the match women's sense of fashion, fun, and camaraderie:

> "They buy their clothes and feathers (especially the latter) by forming clubs; seven or eight of them will join together paying a shilling a week each, and drawing lots to decide who shall have the money each week" (Matchgirls' Memorial, n.d.).

The match production industry was one of the largest in the country, and creating those tiny sticks of wood that provided light to people was dangerous work. Just like in Lowell, Massachusetts, the workforce in the factories of London in the 1880s consisted mostly of women. Many of these women were the daughters, wives, and sisters of Irish immigrants who had come to England to work, often as dockers and gas workers. A few of those Irish immigrants had a direct hand in building the iconic *HMS Titanic*, which set sail in 1912. London's East End became known as "the dark heart of London" due to its high levels of social deprivation, immigration, gang activity, prostitution, and crime. In this chapter, we'll explore the life of Sarah Chapman, a revolutionary hero that changed workers' rights forever by leading the Bryant & May Match Factory Strike of 1888.

British Victorian society tended to stereotype women into two categories: "*The Angel in the House*" after the poem by Coventry Patmore, a highly-idealized notion of the perfect Christian housewife, and "the fallen woman," evident in the painting "The Awakening Conscience" by William Holman Hunt, which reflected the Victorian horror of losing respectability and being shunned by society. Both attitudes were heavily influenced by the prevailing ideas of Christian morality in the Victorian era. The match girls were among the lowest strata of respectable society (Kühl, 2016). The story of the Bryant & May Match Factory Strike coincides with the stories of the world's most notorious serial killer, Jack the Ripper. The strike ended in July 1888, and Jack's first victim, a female prostitute from Whitechapel in London's East End, was found in August of the same year. Jack's heinous crimes were, in his own words, motivated by the general misogyny of the time and his deep personal hatred of women. The match women involved in the strike purportedly received a threatening letter from Jack the Ripper, or somebody claiming to be him, about their rebellion. His crimes reflect how society viewed women as dispensable sexual objects or as a means to an end for the powerful men of the time. They weren't respected as contributing members of society, weren't allowed to express their opinions, and were expected to be obedient and compliant. Despite these gender stereotypes and deplorable treatment of women, out of these Victorian slums emerged an unbreakable force, a concrete wall of solidarity made up of agents of change. The movement of the match workers, led by Sarah Chapman, caught on like wildfire and changed how women were viewed in the workplace forever.

Early Life

Sarah Chapman was born on 31 October 1862 in London, England. Industrialization was in full swing in England by the time Sarah was born, and Sarah's parents, Samuel and Sarah, were working in industrial London to support their family. Sarah's father worked as a brewer's servant in a local brewery. He would be in charge of cleaning the brewing equipment, overseeing the brewing process on the brewery floor, and possibly packaging the alcohol brewed. It's likely that these processes had also become industrial by the time Sarah was born. Sarah's mother and older sister worked as matchmaking machinists at the Bryant & May match factory located in Bow, London.

Sarah had six siblings, four older than her and two younger. Her family lived in a house in Mile End, a bustling hub in London's notorious East End. Sarah lived in the East End her entire life, developing a deep connection to its culture and understanding of the struggles of its immigrant social structure. She experienced the extreme contrasts of wealth in the city, where the poor had to give up their lives to work to ironically "make a living." Mile End was where working-class immigrants made their homes when they arrived in London. It was known as a place where working-class immigrants made their homes when they arrived in London. Sarah would have been exposed to different cultures because of the Irish and Jewish families that settled in the area. Despite the rich culture, there was still the class politics of the time. Immigrants were treated as less important than English citizens, so Sarah would have also witnessed poverty, homelessness, abandoned children after their parents worked to death in the nearby factories, and the discrimination practiced by figures of authority like police and local politicians.

The Chapmans were not wealthy by any degree, but they were deemed successful for a working-class family because they managed to maintain a stable home for their seven children, who were all able to read and write. The family stayed in one house for nine years and moved, as a unit, to another, still in Mile End, where they lived for the next 17 years. This unity was rare for most families of the late 1800s in England; the necessity of working usually ripped families apart. Families immigrating from Ireland or European countries to England to look for work often became separated to live near the factories they worked in. Children had to leave their parents and siblings to find work. Parents were often forced to live in separate boarding houses, depending on the rules of the factory they found employment in. Factory owners wanted to control every aspect of their workers' lives, and landlords exploited the already abusive system. Against the odds, the Chapman family unit survived intact, which made them admirable and unusual among the families of East London.

Sarah's education and stable family life had given her the advantage of a solid foundation, so she could use her natural leadership skills to unify the working-class women of London's East End and mobilize one of the most impactful strikes for workers' rights in history. As a young girl, Sarah was also exposed to the gender discrimination that was rife around the world. Her stable family life gave her a solid foundation, so she could use her intellect and natural leadership skills to unify the working-class women of London's East End. She would use this insight and her respected position as a scholar among the working-class people of East London to mobilize one of the most impactful strikes for workers' rights in history.

East Ender For Life

The people of the East End were hard-working, and getting a job at a factory to make a living was a common goal. The factory system and the culture of obedience entrenched into factory workers influenced every aspect of life in London. It impacted the way people socialized, organized their family lives, and how they thought about politics. The city relied on the capitalist factory system to support its economy, and the factory system was deeply entrenched with the values of the Church, meaning society in London during the 1880s was conservative, hierarchical, and patriarchal. Sarah joined the mostly female workforce on the East End at the age of 19. It was the norm for young working-class women of the time to start their careers in factories as young as 15. Sarah worked at the Bryant & May match factory in Bow, London, with her mother and older sister. She started as a matchmaking machinist, and she was working in the patents department by the age of 26. It was at Bryant & May that Sarah began her mission as an agent of change for workers' rights in London.

Sarah's struggles as a match worker were two-fold. Firstly, the factories in the East End were governed in an oppressive and harsh manner. Match workers were forced to work under some of the worst conditions, as you will read when we go through the events leading up to the strike. Match workers endured sweatshop conditions as casual or short-term workers. Factory owners, including Bryant & May, took advantage of this casual labor system because it meant workers were not protected by the employment laws governing factories. The owners got away with not paying for basic employment benefits like housing and health care, saving them money but leaving the workers vulnerable to abuse. Workers didn't earn enough to improve their living conditions, so the status quo in society remained in favor of the wealthy industrialists.

The second aspect of Sarah's struggle as a factory worker was her gender. Female workers had to deal with misogyny on and off the factory floor. At work, they were sexually harassed, abused, and sometimes even violated by their male supervisors. The streets surrounding the factories were rife with sexual predators, leaving match women and their children vulnerable to exploitation. Finally, after a hard day's work, many of these women returned to violent husbands or fathers. Their supervisors and co-workers took advantage of this by judging them or making inappropriate gestures and comments. *The Little Match Girl* of Han Christian Andersen's tale was a meek and passive victim of a cruel society. By contrast, these real match girls and women were brash and rough around the edges. They were a product of the economic system they existed in, but they did not fit their society's stereotype of the demure and pathetic young girl who endured her suffering silently. This contributed to their approach to the Match Workers' Strike.

Sarah was from a stable home and was educated, but that didn't mean she wasn't exposed to the hardships experienced by her colleagues at Bryant & May. She worked and socialized with the same women who were treated like machinery by the factory system. Sarah progressed to work as a booker in the patents department of the match factory, which was a higher-paying job than working directly to make the matches. Sarah gained the respect of her colleagues through her position at the factory, her leadership qualities, her intellect, and her deep sense of fairness. Her better-paying role didn't prevent Sarah from experiencing the same harsh conditions of factory life, but it gave her a different perspective on the socio-political aspects of the factory system.

It is likely that Sarah was exposed to radical ideas preceding the strike. Workers were allowed certain social liberties like belonging to social clubs where they could organize book clubs, religious meetings, play games, learn music, and manage their finances. Sarah's actions preceding the strike were influenced by members of a socialist organization called the Fabian Society while she worked at the match factory. The group sought social and economic reform through radical left-wing ideals. These ideals included the redistribution of wealth to create a welfare state, universal health care, and the creation of a minimum wage to prevent factory workers from being abused as casual employees. The fact that these ideals resonated with Sarah, and motivated her to make the bold moves she did during the strike, indicates that Sarah had an intrinsic sense of right and wrong about how the workers were being treated at Bryant & May. Karl Marx's daughter, Eleanor Marx-Aveling, helped the match girls organize their strike meetings. Karl Marx's Communist Manifesto was published in 1848 before Sarah was born.

The Bryant & May Match Factory Strike

Manufacturing matches on a large scale was a lucrative business in the 1800s in England and countries across the world. Matches were used in almost every home and every establishment because electricity grids were not yet widely installed in cities. The Bryant & May company employed 5000 workers in their factories by the 1880s. Most of these workers were women and girls from Irish immigrant families as young as 12 and 13, who were forced to work six days a week. Making matches was treacherous and arduous work. The matches started as thin and long wooden sticks. These sticks were slotted into frames in their thousands, with the ends of the sticks exposed on either side of the frame. The frames were then dipped into a potent cocktail of extremely hazardous chemicals. The combination included high amounts of sulfur, powdered glass, and yellow phosphorus. The matchsticks were cut in half after being dipped before being boxed and transported. The average match worker at Bryant & May worked a 10-to-14 hour shift and was expected to complete about 1000 frames of matches in this time. The matches were called *Lucifers* because of the sulfuric smell they emitted when lit. The name was apt because employees were working in hellish conditions.

The match factory was owned by William Bryant and Francis May, both part of the conservative Christian group of settlers known as Quakers. The pair had originally imported red phosphorus-based safety matches from Johan Edvard Lundström, in Sweden, in 1850. As demand for matches rapidly increased, Bryant and May bought Lundström's UK patent, building a match factory in Bow. Red phosphorus was much more expensive than the alternative, which was white phosphorus-based matches. Using child labor available in the areas close to Bow kept production costs down. At its height, the factory employed around 3000 East End children, predominantly girls (Satre, 1982).

Besides the workload being tremendous and involving operating dangerous machinery, the working conditions at Bryant & May were atrocious. The heated yellow phosphorus that the matchsticks were dipped in emitted a potent and poisonous vapor. Workers in charge of dipping the matches into the phosphorus chemical concoction had no choice but to inhale this vapor. Many of them suffered from a terrifying condition known as "phossy jaw" that caused the jaw bone to deteriorate. Many workers were forced to work even though their teeth and jaw were dissolving because of the phosphorus. Workers with phossy jaw were pushed to continue working and threatened with being fired if they wanted to take time off to recover. Supervisors were on the lookout for workers who complained of sore teeth or headaches; they were made to have their teeth removed or risk getting fired. Despite workers suffering terrible facial disfigurements and even fatal brain damage from phossy jaw, the condition was ignored by Bryant & May until the strike brought it to light. Renowned author Charles Dickens wrote about companies being aware of the devastating effects of phossy jaw in his 1852 essay called *One of the Evils of Match-Making*:

> Annie Brown is twenty years of age, of pale and scrofulous aspect. She went to work at the lucifer-factory when she was nine years old, and after she had worked for about four years, the complaint began, like a toothache. At night, she could see that her clothes were glowing on the chair where she had put them; her hands and arms were glowing also... her lower jaw is almost entirely wanting; at the side of her mouth are two or three large holes. The jaw was removed at the Infirmary seven years ago (Dickens, 1852).

As if phossy jaw wasn't nightmare enough, match workers suffered truly heinous working conditions. Factory owners imposed petty fines on the employees' already low wages. They were penalized if they lit matches by accident, had dirty feet or untidy workspaces, dropped matches on the factory floor, or arrived late to work. The workers in charge of putting the matches into boxes had to pay for the glue used to stick the boxes together. Many workers lost fingers and toes because of the dangerous matchmaking machinery they had to operate. Injured workers would often be fined for slowing down production and failing to meet their steep production quotas for the day. Employees had no designated area to eat their meals during the day, and their food was often contaminated with the phosphorus in the atmosphere, causing many workers to fall ill.

The female workers were treated much worse than their male colleagues. They were bullied by their managers, by political leaders in the area who pulled the economic strings, and by local religious leaders who formed part of the factory system of bureaucracy and misogyny. Factory fines were wielded like weapons intended to keep the women submissive and "where they belonged" as lesser than men without any rights or the possibility of progress. Some women endured abusive husbands, fathers, or brothers who bullied them at home. The poorest match girls were living on the streets because of the high cost of living and low factory wages. Birth control was taboo because of the religious oppression of the time, and many women had children they couldn't afford nor had the time to take care of. Others were the sole breadwinners in their homes and still received no respect. It is no surprise that alcoholism was common among workers facing these desperate odds.

Tensions began rising at Bryant & May throughout the 1880s. The company turned a blind eye to reports of phossy jaw and refused to improve working conditions. The political fire of revolution was lit on 15 June 1888 when the Fabian Society encouraged the public to boycott Bryant & May matches to make the company feel the sting in their pocket. This was the first step of many toward change. Later that month, a well-known member of the Fabian Society, social revolutionary, feminist, and writer Annie Besant interviewed women who worked at Bryant & May's Bow factory. The interview resulted in Annie's iconic article titled *White Slavery in London* in her weekly newspaper called *The Link*. Annie's role in the Match Factory Strike will be further explored in the next chapter.

The article caused a media frenzy that centered around the ruthless practices at Bryant & May. Instead of fixing the problems highlighted in the article, the company tried to do damage control. Mr. Bryant even threatened to sue Annie Besant for libel. They demanded that the women who had been interviewed sign a statement denying the truth of the claims described in Annie's article. The women refused to sign the statements, and consequently, a few of them were fired. This was the tinder that caused the strike to light up London's East End.

Sarah Chapman was enraged. On 6th July, Annie received the "Dear Lady" letter stating the following from the match workers about the situation:

> My Dear Lady, - we thank you very much for the kind interest you have taken in us poor girls, and hope that you will succeed in your undertakings. Dear lady, you need not trouble yourself about the letter I read in the Link that Mr. Bryant sent you, because you have spoken the truth, and we are very pleased to read it. Dear lady, they are trying to get the poor girls to say that it is all lies that has been printed, and trying to make them sign papers to say it is lies; dear lady, no one knows what we have to put up with, and we will not sign them. We all thank you very much for the kindness you have shown to us. My dear lady, we hope you will not get into any trouble in our behalf, as what you have spoken is quite true; dear lady, we hope that if there will be any meeting we hope you will let us know it in the book. I have no more to say at present, from yours truly, with kind friends wishes for you, dear lady, for the kind love you have shown us poor girls. Dear lady do not mention the date this letter was written or I might have put my or our names, but we are frightened, do keep that as a secret, we

know you will do that dear lady"(Matchgirls' Memorial, n.d.).

On 5th July 1888, 1,400 female workers walked out of the factory, determined to stand their ground against how the company was treating them. By the 6th of July, the entire factory was empty as workers took to the streets. Sarah was instrumental in leading a march of 200 women through Mile End to Annie Besant's office on the 6th of July 1888 to inform her of the dismissals. Sarah and Annie led the women in forming a Strike Committee to take public action against Bryant & May. The Strike Committee was made up of Sarah, Mary Cummings, Mary Driscoll, Alice Francis, Eliza Martin, Mary Naulls, Kate Sclater, and Jane Wakeling. Sarah and her fellow activists saw an advocate and ally in Annie, and they worked together to achieve their common goal for the match workers. "You stood up for us and we wasn't going to back down on you," the women said to Annie (Johnson, 2018).

The metaphorical fire lit by the Strike Committee continued to rage until the 8th of July. The women caused a sensation by meeting in public to announce their struggles and demands for change. Everyone in Bow would be able to hear the commotion. It was unheard of for women to raise their voices in public protest. The Strike Committee led every step of the way by Sarah, marched to Parliament to explain their cause until they finally got an audience with the directors of Bryant & May to lay down their demands.

On 17 July, from the ashes of the revolutionary fire the Strike Committee had left in their wake, the workers' demands were met by the company. The petty fines imposed on workers were stamped out, and the women fired for refusing to sign the false statements about Annie's article were reinstated. Wages were increased, and workers no longer had to pay for their own materials for packing the matches. The demand for a separate space to eat their lunch was also met, and wheelbarrows were provided so the workers would no longer have to carry heavy packs of boxed matches on their heads. The company agreed to let the workers form a trade union for match workers. The Strike Committee agreed that, in the future, workers would not take any strike action without first reporting their grievances to Bryant & May. Sarah is noted as the leader of the Strike Committee, and her voice and actions, along with Annie Besant's influence, brought about the revolutionary changes of the Match Factory Strike. She was brave enough to walk out of the factory on that sweltering July summer's day, even though factories offered stable employment to alleviate the hellish grinding poverty in the East End of Victorian London. Sarah and her colleagues ensured the strike was a public spectacle in a society where it was unheard of for workers to stand up to their employers and women to stand up to men. The women succeeded for themselves, the match workers of London, and millions of women who would benefit from the cinders of their revolutionary fire for centuries to come.

Sarah's Lasting Impact

Sarah's legacy began as soon as she encouraged those 1400 women to abandon the factory on 6 July 1888. By the end of July, the employment revolution was in full swing, with Bryant & May representing the first major factory employer in England that caved to the demands of its workers. The success of the strike had a ripple effect on the employment landscape in London. Sarah and her fellow Strike Committee leaders helped form the Union of Women Match Makers on 27 July 1888. She was elected as one of the 12 leaders of the trade union and then later elected to join the National Trade Union Congress, a body that represents most trade unions in England. It was an incredible achievement on its own, yet it was more significant because Sarah was a woman from a working-class family. She was given the opportunity to make real changes to the employment laws of the country, and she used this role wisely to vet and approve proposals discussed by the body. Trade union membership continued to increase after the strike, and the awareness about the struggles of the working class in London couldn't be suppressed back into its restrictive matchbox. For example, dock workers took to the streets of England in 1889 during the Great Dock Strike after being influenced by the Matchworkers' Strike. Without Sarah's influence and call for direct action, trade unions might not be as influential as they are today.

By December 1891, Sarah had left her post at Bryant &

May and married carpenter Charles Dearman. They had six children and settled in Bethnal Green, still in London's East End. She died at the age of 83 in 1945 and sadly was buried in an unmarked grave. This lack of recognition is disappointing in light of Sarah's bravery and invaluable contribution to the rights of female workers and organized strike action for Britain and the world. Her grave was intended to be mounded or dug up, and the ground flattened. However, in 2020, Sarah's family, spearheaded by great-granddaughter Samantha Johnson, petitioned Parliament to acknowledge the historical significance of Sarah's gravesite and prevent it from being destroyed. It has not yet been determined whether Sarah's grave will be excavated or left undisturbed and commemorated, but the creators of the *Matchgirls' Memorial* intend to keep Sarah's legacy alive by educating others about her and the matchworkers' stories.

Sarah set a noteworthy example for the younger match girls. Mary Driscoll, another member of the Strike Committee, was only 14-years-old and illiterate at the time of the strike. Her belief in the match workers' cause compelled her to join forces with the likes of Sarah and Annie to fight for her rights. Mary was from a family of Irish immigrants, and at the age of 22, she married Thomas, a violent alcoholic who worked on the docks. After Thomas's death and the death of her baby son, Mary became a shopkeeper to support her young family and continued to voice her political beliefs until her death in 1943. Mary was known for her quiet power, independence, and the respect she commanded within her community. She would encourage this same fighting spirit within her own children by telling them to "Always hold your head up. Remember you're as good as anyone" (Raw, 2011).

Chapter Four

Annie Besant

Match Girls' Advocate, Journalist & Socialist

Better remain silent, better not even think, if you are not prepared to act. —Annie Besant

Sarah Chapman's actions can be likened to the match struck across the surface of the matchbox to ignite the fires of the Match Factory Strike. The actions of our next labor rights icon can be likened to the striking surface itself, providing the method and motivation to light the flame. Annie Besant's story takes us to the belly of the beast of the labor revolution in England in the late 1800s. It was taboo for the "lower classes" to challenge those in power during the Victorian era. The captains of industry were well-respected by the upper classes for bringing wealth and economic opportunities to Great Britain. Charitable organizations played an instrumental role in social care in

Victorian society. The educated women of the Ladies Aid Societies, "the Angel in the House," engaged in charitable works, dispensing charity to the morally-deserving poor, the "Fallen Woman," the implicit subtext being their return or conversion to good Christian morality. The possibility that young, barely literate female factory workers were capable of organizing a syndicate, raising strike funds, and lobbying Members of Parliament by themselves was unheard of. "When the match women came out fighting – loud and proud and showing remarkable solidarity – the middle classes realized they had wildly underestimated them. And so had their employers" (TUC150, 2018). Class politics was the elephant in the room, an open secret that was blissfully ignored by those who benefited from its existence while the real victims of the class divide slogged like slaves in the factories of London. Although Annie Besant was often inaccurately credited as the force behind the strike, as an advocate for change, she was essential to the progress that resulted after the Match Factory Strike.

In this chapter, we'll traverse the halls of secrecy of revolutionary groups, like the Fabian Society, through the lens of Annie's controversial writing and socialist activism. She was a reluctant peace-loving middle-class heroine of the working class, and she had a knack for articulating their struggles in ways they never thought possible. We'll explore Annie's early life, her political affiliations, and her intriguing personal life, both before and after the Match Factory Strike. Annie was at the helm, steering the narrative of the changing perspectives of the working class on politics, social issues, and the economy. Annie wielded her pen like a sword in her fight to have workers' rights acknowledged and formalized by the government of the time.

Early Life

Annie Besant was born Annie Wood in London in 1847. In terms of the class structure of the time, Annie's family was deemed middle-to-upper class because of her heritage. Her father was a son of English politicians, and he went on to become a medical doctor, giving Annie's family prestige in British Victorian society. Annie's mother was Irish and came from a working-class family. Annie's father died when Annie was just five-years-old, and her mother, just like Harriet Hanson's, was left with nothing to support her young family. As a young child, Annie witnessed her mother, Emily, struggle to make ends meet after the loss of her husband until she secured a job managing a boys' school boarding house.

Her mother's inability to afford to keep her daughter is what changed the trajectory of Annie's life. She was placed in the care of Ellen Marryat, a friend of her mother's and a strong independent woman herself. Ellen made Annie's education a priority, and she taught Annie her first concepts about making personal sacrifices for the greater good of society. Ellen also encouraged Annie not to let her thoughts and actions be restricted by gender stereotypes in society. British society was organized on the basis of race, class, and gender. White, wealthy males occupied the highest pedestal. Women were not highly regarded in any social, political, or economic sphere other than as wives and objects of male affection (i.e., another form of property to own). Ellen's influence on Annie's upbringing was inflammatory, and by the end of her teenage years, she was ready to take on the establishment and become, in their eyes, a troublemaker.

Annie married Frank Besant when she was just 20 years old. Frank was a member of the clergy of the Anglican Church. On the surface, the couple were compatible because Annie came from a staunch Anglican background, and their views aligned for the most part. However, this marital bliss would soon change at Annie's behest. Despite her gender, Annie's social standing allowed her to socialize with educated men of her class, and through these social interactions, she met radical reformists who brought the struggles of the working-class men and women working in industrial London to her attention.

Annie became increasingly frustrated by the amount of influence the Church had over the government. She made the connection between the fact that many factory owners were, or had descended from, conservative Christian families, to the way religion influenced how they ran their factories. She began to see Frank being part of the Church as a moral contradiction she could no longer live with, and they separated even though divorce was social suicide. Annie's middle-class status helped her avoid being treated as a pariah by her peers, and the couple was technically still married but living separately.

Annie choosing to sever ties with Frank represented her liberation from the shackles of gender stereotypes and religious oppression, which had been holding her back from becoming an agent for change in her community. This free spirit now threw her energy into writing. She educated herself about secularism and the political ideas associated with communism, socialism, and democracy. The struggles of the working class occupied more and more space in Annie's mind until she decided to do something about the situation. Her thoughts were truly free, and she used this freedom to gather the kindling that would start the political fire of labor reform through the Match Factory Strike of 1888.

Radical Feminism Takes Hold

The formation of Annie's political views, and desire to bring about change, can be tracked through the major events in her life. Her passion for women's rights might have originated in her mother's financial struggles as a widow, to the point of separating the family in order to give her child a better chance in life. In Emily's dilemma, Annie saw reflected the plight of women everywhere without economic recourse of their own. Her guardian's teachings influenced her to view women's rights as non-negotiable and that all citizens deserved certain inalienable rights. The feminist inside Annie was further motivated by the oppression she experienced as a woman married to a member of the clergy. The state and the Church were both parties to their marriage, and this didn't sit well with Annie's liberal viewpoint. Her failed marriage left her questioning her faith regarding the politics of the day. As she got deeper into the secularist movement by becoming a prominent member of the Secular Society, she saw the contradiction of trying to create a fair and just society through the lens of religion. On a personal level, Annie felt the sting of misogyny woven into the fabric of society because she wasn't able to profit from her writing while she was married to Frank since married women weren't allowed to own property, and this included intellectual property. Annie wanted to associate with like-minded people willing to advocate for the freedom and independence of all social classes.

Annie's career as an activist for social, political, and economic reform came after she separated from Frank Besant. She began living with Charles Bradlaugh, a friend of hers who was also liberal-minded and a writer. They made a formidable pair and created much controversy leading up to the 1880s. Annie's intention to highlight the evils of the divide between social classes was clear when she worked with Charles in 1877 to publish a book titled The Fruits of Philosophy, which argued that birth control would allow the working class and the poorest in society to prosper by giving them control over their family dynamics. Advocating for birth control was considered deplorable, and the hint that women's sexuality could have a pleasurable instead of merely reproductive function was deeply disturbing for the time because the Church promoted conservative ideals. Any suggestion of the elevation of the working class was equally frowned upon, as it was not in the interests of the rich capitalists pulling the purse strings of the country. Entrepreneurs needed their workers to remain poor and hungry to keep them coming back to work to line the employers' already full pockets. Another reason the book was controversial was that it suggested that women should have a say in their sexual activities instead of just complying and giving birth to as many children as possible.

Annie and Charles's decision to publish such a book placed Annie on the radar of those whose task it was to uphold the oppressive status quo. Her attitude and unwavering dedication to her beliefs raised more red flags than Charles's actions because she was a woman. Despite those in power trying to silence their controversial opinions, the pair's reformist sentiments were largely supported by the British public because they elected Charles to be an MP in 1880. This election made Annie a high-profile activist, and she was catapulted into a position of relative power to be the voice of the oppressed, despite her gender.

In 1887, Annie intended to speak at a public meeting to bring awareness to the high levels of unemployment that affected mostly Irish immigrants in London. Chaos ensued at Trafalgar Square, London, and turned into the riot and famous event of police brutality known as Bloody Sunday. Annie's writings and public statements leading up to the protest led her to be blamed for inciting the crowd to challenge the police. The police surrounded the crowd and arrested many of the protestors, to whom Annie later provided legal assistance.

Her education, life experiences, and socialization made Annie continue to question, prod, and poke at societal norms in every space she occupied. She was almost expelled from the Birkbeck Literary and Scientific Institute when she spouted secularist and anti-capitalist rhetoric on her examination papers and through her lively social interactions. Once again, the powers at the Institute tried to silence Annie by sealing her examination answer papers, but she was undeterred. It's as if every attempt to keep her quiet added another splash of gasoline to the fire brewing within Annie to make a bold statement about how society needed to improve to benefit the downtrodden. She began to furiously write about what she observed and wrote controversial columns in national newspapers about the danger of failing to untether society and politics from the influence of the Church. Her views and social commentary on class politics culminated in her writing her own weekly newspaper called *The Link,* where she shed light on how the working class was being abused by the capitalist system. As previously mentioned, her article called *White Slavery* in London published in June 1888, was the first spark that ignited the flames of unrest that culminated in the Match Factory Strike and its after effects.

Annie Was The Link!

Annie was a significant member of the Fabian Society; a revolutionary group that worked on introducing socialist reforms into an imbalanced capitalist system where the scales of justice were tipped in favor of the wealthy elite. Annie used her self-published articles in *The Link* to highlight the various hardships experienced by the working class. Because of her social class and social awareness, Annie knew of the dangerous work the match women were subjected to. She was instrumental in the Fabian Society's highly publicized boycott of Bryant & May match products in June 1888. Society members hoped that the boycott would hurt the greedy factory owners in their pockets.

Annie's position of privilege compared to the match women involved in the strike gave her a view of the bigger picture from both sides. She was able to observe how the upper class benefited from the ill-treatment of the match workers through her social and political interactions with women of the elite class. These women included those of the various charity organizations run by the sophisticated wives, mothers, and sisters of wealthy aristocrats who were directly or indirectly exploiting the working class. The women would hold performative charity events to raise funds for those less privileged without actually taking any real action to change the status quo. Because of their position in society and their affiliation with the Church, the women were praised for their empty gestures. Annie refused to stand back and watch these privileged women have convoluted discussions about what the women on the streets of the East End were going through. She decided to interview a few of the female match workers to gain a more meaningful perspective.

The interview revealed the horrific details of daily life for the average match worker at Bryant & May. Annie's *White Slavery in London* article put into words the stark realities faced by young girls and women. She described how they had to work unreasonably long hours, stand for their entire workday, be paid less than a living wage, pay for matches lit by accident, and how the girls were brainwashed into being grateful for the abuse they were subjected to in the form of employment. The dangerous nature of matchmaking, and the unfair penalty system at the factory, were also explained in detail in the article. "One girl was fined 1s. for letting the web twist round a machine in the endeavor to save her fingers from being cut, and was sharply told to take care of the machine, 'never mind your fingers'" (Besant, 1888). The horrors of being exposed to white phosphorus were also described in the article. Annie detailed how the workers had to eat their lunch amidst the phosphorus fumes in the poorly ventilated factory, leaving many of them nauseous and violently ill:

> Do you know that girls are used to carrying boxes on their heads until the hair is rubbed off and the young heads are bald at fifteen years of age? Country clergymen with shares in Bryant and May's, draw down on your knee your fifteen year old daughter; pass your hand tenderly over the silky beauty of the black, shining tresses (Besant, 1888).

Annie emphasized the unfairness of the situation by comparing the profits made by Bryant & May to what they paid and fined their workers. Another important issue that Annie raised in her article was that the directors of Bryant & May had forced the match women to give up the wages they would have earned from their workday to help put up a statue of William Gladstone, a popular politician at the time. She highlighted that the directors were making a huge profit by exploiting the match workers and that no one in society cared enough to do anything to help the workers. She bravely recorded that the working conditions at Bryant & May were a form of slavery and unacceptable to treat fellow human beings in such an inhumane manner for the sake of profit.

> "But who cares for the fate of these white wage slaves? Born in slums, driven to work while still children, undersized because underfed, oppressed because helpless, flung aside as soon as worked out, who cares if they die or go on the streets provided only that the Bryant and May shareholders get their 23 per cent?" (Besant, 1888).

Once the factory's health and safety violations became public, the match that would shed light on the struggles of match workers around the country was lit. The company's directors were so outraged by her article that they asked the women interviewed to sign statements saying that what they told Annie wasn't true. Those who refused were fired, and as discussed in the previous chapter, this injustice triggered Sarah Chapman to mobilize the match workers to abandon the factory. Annie had no idea that Sarah Chapman and her 1,400 colleagues had walked out of the factory in Bow until they showed up outside her office door on 6th July 1888. Far from being the instigator of the strike, Annie was reluctant to advise the match workers to engage in strike action because she feared what the loss of income might mean for their survival. It seems more likely that the match women convinced Annie to help them set up a Strike Committee to have their demands heard by the highest powers.

Annie was a social campaigner who never backed down from a cause she truly believed in. She supported the match women until their demands were met on 17 July 1888. Throughout the progression of the Match Factory Strike, Annie continued to publish subversive letters and correspondence between her and the lawyers representing Bryant & May. The company was intent on suing Annie for her *White Slavery in London* article. Annie publicly dismissed their attacks and encouraged them to challenge the truth of any of the statements made in her article about working conditions at the factory. Annie's support of the match women was unwavering, and together, they made sure that every demand for change at the factories was met. Bryant & May was the giant of the matchmaking industry, so if they could be defeated by strike action, every other smaller match company could be too. It was a major step forward for socialist reform in the harshly capitalist landscape of industrial London.

Other notable activists lent their support and got involved in the strike. These include suffragist Emmeline Pankhurst as she notes in her autobiography entitled *My Own Story*:

> I threw myself into this strike with enthusiasm, working with the girls and with some women of prominence, amongst these the celebrated Mrs Annie Besant... It was a time of tremendous unrest, of labour agitations, of strikes and lockouts. It was a time also when a most stupid reactionary spirit seemed to take possession of the Government and the authorities (Pankhurst, 1914).

Trade unionist Henry Snell also recorded his observations about the strike in his book *Men, Movements, and Myself*:

> These courageous girls had neither funds, organizations, nor leaders, and they appealed to Mrs. Besant to advise and lead them. It was a wise and most excellent inspiration... The number affected was quite small, but the matchgirls' strike had an influence upon the

minds of the workers which entitles it to be regarded as one of the most important events in the history of labour organisation in any country (Snell, 1936).

Other notable figures in society who supported Annie Besant's campaign to improve working conditions of the match workers were William Stead, the editor of the Pall Mall Gazette, writer George Bernard Shaw and William and Catharine Booth of the Salvation Army.

Annie's Legacy

After the Match Factory Strike, Annie rode the wave of the political revolution she and the other match women had brought to crash on London. She played an important role in the Great Dock Strike of 1889, where she helped the dock worker representatives articulate the rules they wanted the dockworkers' union to encompass. She helped to organize, publicize, and mobilize the strike action so that the workers' demands were met by the docking companies. The success and impact of the Match Factory Strike was unprecedented in England. It would not have been possible without Annie's influence and essential observations about how the class divide meant some people were treated better than others and why this was unacceptable. Annie was the first woman on the London School Board for Tower Hamlets. The working class saw her as a hero, and the wealthy elite saw her as a troublemaker, a characteristic that Annie was aware of and grateful for because it meant she could make real changes.

The final phase of Annie's life took her to India, where she continued to influence her community and those in power with her writing. She spoke publicly about her desire for the country to become a democracy and her personal transformation after being introduced to Theosophy. Theosophy is a philosophy that encourages its followers to discover and connect with God spiritually through gaining knowledge and personal introspection. She continued to campaign for women's rights through her membership in the International Order of Freemasonry for Men and Women, where she was allowed to make an impact equal to the male members of the organization.

She openly encouraged the Indian public to abandon their social hierarchies of the caste system by promoting the benefits of educating women and girls to uplift the entire community. Annie was personally involved in many of the lives of her students during her time in India as the president of the Theosophical Society, and she advocated for the country to adopt a democratic system of government. She passed away in 1933 at the age of 85. From the beginning of her life, Annie strived to bring out the best in humanity by shedding the prejudices we hold based on what makes us different. She focused her life's work on uplifting people based on what humans have in common, which is their humanity. She laughed in the face of controversy and those who challenged her because she had an inherent sense of right and wrong based on what she observed in life. Her unwavering compassion, commitment to peace, and willingness to sacrifice her personal comfort to bring awareness to the suffering of her fellow man are what makes Annie a trailblazer for the women who continued the fight after her.

In 1963, a blue plaque was placed at Annie's former home in Gypsy Hill to commemorate her achievements as a social reformer and activist for workers and women's rights. Another blue plaque was unveiled in 2022 in Bow, London, where the entrance of the Bryant & May factory used to be, to commemorate the Match Factory Strike and its achievement in the development of workers' rights and the bravery of the women involved. The match girls have been commemorated in popular culture including the appearance of the character Enola as a match girl in the Netflix movie *Enola Holmes 2*. In 2012, a memorial was commissioned for London's Olympic Park with a poem by Poet Laureate Lemn Sissay etched into it called *The Spark Catchers*. A 2022 novel called *The Little Match Girl Strikes Back* by Emma Carroll and illustrated by Lauren Child is an empowering feminist reworking of the Hans Christian Andersen tale, in which the starving match-selling waif leads the match factory workers out on strike and seizes control of her fate through unity.

The bold acts of another group of brave women across the pond in the U.S. are the focus of our next chapter. The Atlanta Washerwomen Strike brought to light the plight of African-American women, also in the 1880s.

Chapter Five
THE WASHING AMAZONS
THE ATLANTA WASHERWOMEN STRIKE

Black women – then and now – are no strangers to facing resistance when they fight for justice, and Black women – then and now – don't give up easy. —Elizabeth Warren

The Atlanta Washerwomen Strike tells the story of a group of six brave women who stood up for their rights at great personal risk. Its setting is the bustling hub of Atlanta, Georgia, during the sweltering summer of 1881. In the late 1800s, the southern state of Atlanta was on the brink of becoming the cultural hub of great American food, music, and fashion that we know today. The American Civil War had recently ended in 1865, and slavery was officially abolished, leading the country into the postbellum period of the Reconstruction era. This era saw the southern states attempt to economically and politically reintegrate themselves into the rest of the U.S. after the Civil War and slavery.

Atlanta was trying to procure new business from the North to position itself as the golden star of the South with a booming economy. Slavery might have been outlawed, but the economy of Atlanta was still being built off the backs of the African-American community, who were viewed as a cheap source of labor. The majority of these laborers were African-American women who were recently emancipated slaves. The women and their families had moved to the city from rural Georgia to look for work as an opportunity to build a better life after slavery. Major political, social, and economic reform for African-Americans was still a century away because the Civil Rights Movement would only reach lawmakers in the 1960s. Racism was still alive and well in the southern states, and the Atlanta City Council used the ashes of the civil war as leverage to abuse the African-American workforce who now had the chance to uplift their lives and their communities.

The reach of the fashion industry across the country and the availability of synthetic cloth used to make clothing had increased after the Civil War; people now had wardrobes full of clothes that needed washing regularly. The laundry industry soon became one of the largest informal labor industries in the city and it was dominated by hard-working African-American women. Traditionally, laundry was a job or chore reserved for women. These women trained their daughters in the laundry processes. White men did not do their own laundry if they could help it because it was seen as women's work and, therefore, beneath them. White women also preferred to pay to have their family's laundry done because the postbellum South regarded white women as much higher up the social hierarchy compared to Black women. Steam-powered laundry machines, automated laundry services, and household washing machines were non-existent in the southern states in the 1800s. Laundry had to be done by hand, and girls as young as 14 were working as washerwomen in Atlanta. The strike that occurred in the summer of 1881, steered by the Washerwomen, would forever change the way African-American female workers were perceived by Southern society.

What Led to the Strike?

Being a laundress in the 1800s meant backbreaking work. The women had to carry heavy loads of soiled or wet clothes, heat their irons using fire and carry heavy buckets of water. Scrubbing clothes was a difficult task that could take hours. The laundered clothes had to be delivered to their client's homes. Laundresses made their own soap, which was often harmful to their skin. Their clients were mostly white families within the Atlanta community, some of whom still believed they were entitled to free Black labor and begrudgingly paid the laundresses for their hard work. This resulted in the washerwomen earning between

$1 and $2 per week, or $4 to $8 per month. These wages were way below a living wage and a form of economic slavery, despite the women being emancipated. The women were once again managing the households of white families, a task that harked back to the atrocious time when slavery was accepted.

On the other hand, there were certain benefits to being a laundress that other domestic professions couldn't offer. The washerwomen had the freedom and flexibility to work independently and build their own laundry businesses from their homes without having to meet the quotas of a racist and oppressive employer. Laundress Sarah Hill once said, "I could clean my hearth good and nice and set my irons in front of the fire and iron all day [with]out stopping... I cooked and ironed at the same time" (AFL-CIO, n.d.). This sense of autonomy and ownership of their means of earning a living had a significant impact on the confidence of these women, given the recent transition from the chokehold of slavery in Atlanta. More African-American women worked as laundresses than in any other domestic profession and even outnumbered the male casual laborers in Atlanta at the time of the strike. The washerwomen's work was outsourced and self-managed. They had the opportunity to create legacy wealth that they could hand down to their daughters when they retired.

The laundresses had successfully monopolized the laundry industry in Georgia, and the services they provided allowed the wealthy elite to perform their tasks and jobs in the city and have their clothes attended to by experts. Despite their importance within Atlanta's economy, the washerwomen were treated as if their hard work and expertise did not justify them being paid at least a living wage. The white families they provided services to did not want the women to prosper because of the racist fear of the emergence of an African-American middle class with more wealth than them. The laundresses began to get frustrated at how they were treated and their client's refusal to accept a fee increase. The women wanted to maintain their independence and the ownership of their means of production while having a minimum fee for laundry legalized by the Atlanta City Council to give their industry some security and room to grow.

The Atlanta washerwomen's demands weren't new. There had been previous strikes organized by laundresses based on similar demands for increased pay in Mississippi in 1867. The Mississippi washerwomen petitioned to earn a living wage based on the amount of work they were doing, just like their future counterparts in Atlanta. The Mississippi strike resulted in the formation of the first trade union in Mississippi called the Washerwomen of Jackson. However, that strike was given minimal attention by the press. The Atlanta Washerwomen Strike of 1881 had a far greater impact on the larger political consciousness of the African-American workforce in the South.

The touch-paper that ignited the strike in 1881 was the upcoming International Cotton Exposition that summer. The exposition was like a convention or fair that would bring about 200,000 visitors to Atlanta from the North to look for roots to plant their businesses in the South. It was a major opportunity for the city to showcase its potential as a financial beacon of unity between the North and the South. The Atlanta government wanted to continue to exploit its cheap labor source while growing Atlanta's economic profile. They promoted the city by advertising Atlanta's mostly African-American workforce to potential investors as compliant and grateful workers who were happy to do the more labor-intensive jobs that were beneath the dignity of the white population. The workforce was positioned as affordable labor for the wealthy elite to exploit, so their businesses could grow while keeping costs at a minimum. The workers were portrayed as desperate for opportunity after being emancipated at the end of the Civil War. The government of Atlanta chose this racist angle for the exposition and turned a blind eye to the blatant discrimination the washerwomen were subject to, as well as their subsistence wages.

The laundresses, for their part, saw the exposition as an opportunity to put an end to the exploitation of African-American washerwomen in Atlanta. They knew that the city would be buzzing with activity during the exposition, and the visitors from the North would expect their laundry to be done well and fast. A strike would tarnish Atlanta's reputation with the fancy Northern investors and put pressure on the Atlanta City Council. A group of 20 washerwomen met at church in Summerhill on 20 July 1881. They discussed their frustration at their customers refusing to accept their increased laundry fees and that the only way they could earn more money was by increasing their already hefty workload and number of clients. They wanted to formally and legally increase the rates for laundry across Atlanta to $1 per 12 pounds of washing done. These 20 women formed a trade union called the Washing Society to formalize their demands and approach other washerwomen to join their campaign.

Washing Away Racial Oppression

The 20 members of the Washing Society decided to take to the streets of Georgia with their proposal. They knocked on the doors of the other washerwomen they knew within their communities to ask them to join the campaign for a laundry fee increase. The women used public and communal spaces like churches, schools, and recreational areas to meet with other laundresses and give speeches about their campaign to take control of Atlanta's laundry industry. The 20 initial members of the Washing Society grew to more than 3,000 within three weeks of the first meeting because of the tireless campaigning by each member to spread the word about the proposed strike. A small percentage of the Washing Society included white women who worked as laundresses and probably immigrated from Ireland to look for opportunities in the U.S. The Washing Society held weekly meetings where they discussed, strategized, and prayed about their plans to put the Atlanta City Council and their uncooperative racist clients through the proverbial wringer. The impact the strike had on the city's workers is noted in the quote below:

> White employers scrambled to find workers to fill the laundry gap as they feared the strike would spread to other industries. And spread it did: Black waiters at the National Hotel in downtown Atlanta refused to work until their bosses raised their wages — and they won. That scene repeated itself in kitchens, nurseries and sculleries across the city (Kelly, 2022).

The strike began in late July of 1881. The washerwomen employed strategies that attacked the heart of the Atlanta community and brought the city to a near standstill as the Cotton Exposition drew nearer. The laundresses went out of their way to inconvenience the white households that refused to pay the increased fee. If a client refused to pay the fee, the washerwomen would send back their laundry wet or unwashed. The strike didn't take the women to the streets in protest or have any direct action. Instead, the strike was incorporated into the daily lives of Atlantians who needed clean clothes to go to their jobs but had no time to wash their clothes on their own. The strike severely disrupted business and general life in Atlanta, which was a hub of economic activity in the South. "Southern black women's labor stood on the periphery of the burgeoning economy in the new South, but their work was essential to its effective functioning. Few events in history would demonstrate this more profoundly than the washerwomen's strikes" (Hunter, 1999). The action placed pressure on the government, which was getting increasingly nervous about its supposedly subservient African-American workforce not being on their best behavior for the upcoming visitors.

The *Atlanta Constitution* was a pro-government newspaper that provided extensive coverage of the strike through the lens of the racist white media that swayed public opinion about the women. Atlanta society was still reeling from having to pay former slaves for services they used to be entitled to by owning people as slaves. They were not quick to accept African-Americans, let alone African-American women standing up to the racist establishment and making demands for their own benefit. The bravery of the washerwomen is astounding, considering the existence of the Black Codes and the Jim Crow Laws of the South that made it legal to oppress African-Americans. These racist laws even justified the murder of many innocent African-Americans for speaking out about political injustices. In this context, it's even more frustrating that the *Atlanta Constitution* chose to label the women of the Washing Society as "amazons." This was a derogatory and racist description of the women to take away their value as Americans and as women. As documented in the *Atlanta Constitution* at the time: "The Washerwomen's strike is assuming vast proportions and despite the apparent independence of the white people, is causing quite an inconvenience among our citizens" (Hurt, 2023).

Despite the biased media coverage, the washerwomen continued to defy both the gender and racial expectations of the day by continuing with their strike, and they met regularly to strategize further. By August, the impact of the strike was becoming unmanageable for Atlanta. The City Council agreed to allow the women to unionize and legalize their increased fees under certain conditions. They had to pay a steep annual fee of between $25 and $50 to the City Council to be a formal member of the Washing Society and obtain a license fee to be a laundress. This fee amounted to twice the amount that the average washerwoman earned per year. On top of this condition, the City Council was willing to offer entrepreneurs an exemption from paying taxes if they opened commercial steam-powered laundry businesses to compete with and drive the washerwomen out of business.

The conditions spurred the washerwomen to resist even further, with many abandoning their laundry businesses until their demands were met. During this time, some laundry clients agreed to pay the increased fees; this was deemed a success by the Washing Society. The pressure continued to mount until the Atlanta police intervened on day 10 of the strike by arresting six prominent members of the Washing Society. The six women were charged and heavily fined for their involvement in leading the strike. Their influence will be discussed further in the coming paragraphs. The police claimed that the Washing Society was threatening laundresses into joining their fight. This was untrue and indicated the pressure the strike placed on the government.

The strike continued to inconvenience and frustrate the white families of Atlanta, who depended on the African-American workforce to keep their households running smoothly. The white women of these households did not want to take on the arduous task of doing the family's laundry. The media and the general public dismissed the washerwomen's demands as unreasonable, especially since they were African-American laborers who Atlanta society expected to be grateful to even have a business. The Washing Society refused to back down. On 3 August 1881, the women wrote an open letter to the mayor of Atlanta, Jim English, stating they were willing to pay the annual membership fee of $25 to $50 to get a laundress license. The letter included the following powerful statement that inspired others in the washerwomen community to stand their ground:

> We can afford to pay these licenses, and will do it before we will be defeated, and then we will have full control of the city's washing at our own prices, as the city has control of our husbands' work at their prices. Don't forget this. We hope to hear from your council Tuesday morning. We mean business this week or no washing (Social History for Every Classroom, n.d.).

The City Council eventually dropped their threats of the license fee out of sheer shock at the tenacity of the washerwomen. The government was afraid of the potential backlash and protest action if they decided to go through with their threat. The strike was an outright success, and the washerwomen, for the most part, could collect higher fees for their work while still keeping their autonomy in their businesses.

Consequences of the Strike

The momentum of the strike didn't stop with the washerwomen. The strike had caused a public spectacle, and discomfort of the white population that exploited the African-American workforce was palpable amidst the muggy Atlanta summer of 1881. Their clothes were dirty, and they had lost control over a group of people that they could previously buy and sell as they wanted. The balance of power and status quo had shifted completely after the washerwomen succeeded in getting the city to back down from its threats to impose licensing fees. As Black history research, Jahdziah St. Julien notes about the strike:

> The outcome of the washerwomen's strike was threefold. First, it established black women's incredible capacity to mobilize en masse using grassroots strategies. Second, it interrupted business as usual, leading to media attention, changes in consumer behavior,

and higher wages. And finally, it encouraged other black workers to seek improved conditions and pay; maids, cooks, hotel workers, and nurses began pressuring their employers for better wages (St. Julien, 2020).

Word spread about the upcoming International Cotton Exposition and its importance to the white elite of the city. Collective action and solidarity were the orders of the day when African-American hotel employees, domestic workers, cooks, and housekeepers across Atlanta decided to band together and ask for an increase in their wages. If these employees abandoned their jobs and took to the streets to strike, Atlanta would be brought to its knees, and the potential investment from the exposition would never happen. The disruption to business in Atlanta would be impossible to claw back from. The City Council decided to give in to many of these employees' demands for better treatment and higher wages.

The actions and mobilization of the Atlanta washerwomen didn't tip the scales of justice in favor of the African-American workforce but it was a step in balancing the scales that had always been tipped in favor of their white and wealthy employers. The washerwomen demanded better treatment, and their bravery gained them economic control over the laundry industry in Atlanta. They kept their independence and took a stance that forced the government to see them as more than cheap labor who were still slaves in the aftermath of the Civil War. These former slaves had chosen to emancipate themselves from the economic shackles placed on them by becoming an irreplaceable part of the working class in the New South. The wealthy elite knew that crossing the workers who kept the embers of the city's industries burning would threaten Atlanta's economy and future as a whole. Tera Hunter is a Princeton University historian who is an expert on Black women in the postbellum era. She writes in her book called *To Joy My Freedom: Southern Black Women's Lives and Labors After the Civil War*. "The "Washing Amazons" as they were also known, managed to execute a strike that was "the largest and most impressive among Black Atlantans during the late nineteenth century" (Hunter, 1999).

The Collective Six

The six women arrested on day 10 of the strike were Dora Jones, Matilda Crawford, Sarah Collier, Sallie Bell, Orphelia Turner, and Carrie Jones. These women accurately represented the general demographic of the washerwomen impacted by the low fees paid for laundry services. They were hard-working mothers with large families to support. Most of the washerwomen had survived slavery and wanted to earn a living to try and make ends meet and possibly sew the early seeds of generational wealth for their children. Their work as laundresses was informal and unregulated. The law was still inherently racist, despite the outcome of the Civil War, so there was no government funding to support them if they became unemployed. This display of racism was shown by the *Atlanta Constitution* reporting on the "six ebony-hued damsels" charged with disorderly conduct and fined for allegedly visiting other women's houses and threatening them to join the strike (Hurt, 2023).

When word spread about the regular meetings of the Washing Society and its rapid growth in membership to more than 3,000 in three weeks, the six leaders became a threat to white supremacy in Atlanta. Police arrested and charged them with disorderly conduct and quarreling for recruiting new Washing Society members by going door-to-door and explaining their cause. The media depicted them in a racist manner, and they were portrayed as subversive activists protesting the aspects of Atlanta that made it great for the white population.

Upon their arrest, the women were instructed to pay hefty fines of $5 each, equal to a month's worth of their laundry fees. Sarah Collier was charged and given the option to pay a $20 fine or join a chain gang, a form of punishment where prisoners were chained together and forced to perform intense physical labor. Sarah was 49 years old, had two children, and was a chronic asthmatic. Despite the odds stacked against her, she refused to pay the fines imposed and served in the chain gang for 40 days. This act of bravery was a clear indication of the washerwomen's fearlessness and persistence about their right to a fair wage.

The Atlanta washerwomen took ownership of the laundry industry and contributed to the African-American female workforce experiencing a "growth of their working class consciousness and solidarity" (Hunter, 1999). The Washing Society was organized and reached deep into their own community at a grassroots level to gain organic support for their cause. Their actions and the support they received showed that domestic work was a political issue. The women leveraged their nuanced understanding of the racial politics they lived in and how this contributed to the respect they received for their work from the government and white households they served. They tossed aside the idea of being grateful for the work they were given by the white population, and rode the wave of the recent emancipation of the African-American community to bring about meaningful changes. They highlighted the importance of African-American people to the security of the American economy, especially in the New South. The economy of Atlanta could not progress without the cooperation of the African-American (mostly female) workforce. The washerwomen used this fact to fight for the rights of that workforce. They took symbolic torches to the laundry they worked so hard to keep clean and refused to cower when threatened by the government. These women were trailblazers because they claimed their rightful power over the means of production they needed to make a living.

Discrimination based on race and gender continued long after the strike occurred, and it would take decades for women to get the right to vote. However, the washerwomen of Atlanta took a step in the right direction, a direction that was previously uncharted by emancipated African-Americans to the extent achieved by the Washing Society. Laundry workers continued to fight for their rights through strikes in the early 1990s across the South because they were inspired by the actions of the washerwomen. Trade unions, workers' organizations, and mass strike actions were inspired to mobilize the African-American workforce to show the racist governments still trying to oppress them that they were not going to be a compliant and abused workforce any longer. Our next fiery female is Lucy Parsons, a radical activist who took inspiration from the bravery of the Atlanta washerwomen.

Chapter Six

LUCY PARSONS

The Goddess of Anarchy

Let us sink such differences as nationality, religion, politics, and set our eyes eternally and forever toward the rising star of the industrial republic of labor. —Lucy Parsons

Lucy Parsons provides the next trailblazing tale on our journey of progress for women's and workers' rights in the U.S. after the Civil War. Lucy wasn't directly involved in the Atlanta Washerwomen Strike of 1881, but she was likely deeply inspired by the bravery and achievements of the legendary laundresses. Lucy was laser-focused on the plight of the working class, their lack of awareness of their true collective power, and the dangers of letting capitalism continue to pull the strings of politics, society, and the economy. Lucy was making her own political waves in the same era as the Atlanta washerwomen on the east coast in Chicago, Illinois, where she risked her life to publicly denounce capitalism at every chance she got.

Seen as a radical instigator for her anarchist views, Lucy threw caution to the wind in her career as a fierce political activist. She was an anarchist who saw capitalism as the root cause of the mistreatment and oppression of the working class and women. She framed her entire outlook on the problems in the society she lived in through the lens of the working class. Lucy openly shared her opinion that the only way to uplift the working class was to overthrow the oppressive economic regime of capitalism. She advocated eliminating the concept of a ruling class to oppress those they decided belonged to classes beneath them.

Early Life

Lucy's early life is unique, and her actions as an activist should be considered in this context. Lucy stepped into controversy from the moment she was born Lucia Carter in Virginia in 1853. She was born a slave, and it is likely that her owner was also her father. The horrific and sadly typical abuse Lucy's mother was subjected to is the stuff of nightmares. Times were changing when Lucy was born, and the path leading to the abolishment of slavery in 1861 had been carved in the dusty dirt roads of the rural southern states. As if he wasn't vile enough, Lucy's owner or master wanted to evade the abolition movement and moved deeper into the South to Waco, Texas, where he was able to retain Lucy and her mother as his property.

Texas was seen as a state of opportunity and development for African-Americans from the Southern States. They could look for work and join active political groups making progress, despite the stench of racism and slavery lingering like humidity in the Texas air. Lucy did what was expected of her as the daughter of a slave in Texas by taking on odd jobs as a seamstress and cook for local white families. The irony of expecting African-American women to work in white households while being treated as subhuman might have been the tiny spark that lit the fire of activism that began to bubble within Lucy as she grew up. Before she could come to grips with her circumstances, Lucy was palmed off to a much older man who was a former slave when she was just a teenager. They lived together, and Lucy gave birth to a baby who died after living for only a few months. The tragedy of Sudden Infant Death Syndrome (SIDS) was sadly common.

Lucy's life would change forever when she met Albert Parsons in 1871. A journalist and newspaper editor, he had abandoned his post as a Confederate soldier to run for political office. The relationship was controversial and frowned upon by the people of Texas. The fact that the couple was interracial caused much public outrage, and a Confederate veteran being romantically involved with a slave, poured gasoline on the fire of prejudice the couple was subjected to. Tired of the scrutiny, the couple packed up and decided to move to the more liberal-minded city of Chicago, Illinois, in 1873. As the couple blew into the Windy City, they were officially married due to interracial marriage being briefly permitted. Lucy took the opportunity to abandon her literal and figurative shackles by refusing to take on the jobs stereotypically reserved for African-American women, like being a laundress, housekeeper, or cook for white families. She wanted to be a writer, so she rebranded herself as Lucy Parsons. This phoenix-like rising from the ashes of her past linked to slavery and hardship set the stage for Lucy to change the future with her radical ideals.

Anarchy Takes Hold

She may not have wanted to be a cook, but Lucy certainly found ways to stir the political pot in Chicago. She and Albert witnessed the brutality of the government's military force against protesting railroad workers in the Great Railroad Strike of 1877, and it changed their views forever. They decided to become anarchists after seeing the carnage of the protests, and her unwavering belief in this ideology would make Lucy the fiery female we know her as today.

The perception of anarchy might be one of lawlessness, disorder, and chaos, but Lucy saw the concept as a vehicle for hope among the working class. In Lucy's own words, "Anarchists are peaceable, law-abiding people. What do anarchists mean when they speak of anarchy? Webster gives the term two definitions: chaos and the state of being without political rule. We cling to the latter definition. Our enemies hold that we believe only in the former" (Black Past, 2007). Her views began to form around the spectrum of anarchism, socialism, and absolute democracy. At the center of this spectrum lay the struggles of the working class, whose odds were poor when stacked against those of the wealthy capitalist elite.

Lucy believed that anarchy was the cure for the disease of capitalism that had spread across America and infected the working class with poverty, ignorance, and complacency. It was a belief she vehemently defended throughout her political career. She articulated these radical ideas through her career as a labor organizer and journalist for subversive and controversial publications like *The Social* and *The Alarm*, the latter of which her husband Albert was the editor. Lucy believed there was no military or political power strong enough to overpower the will of the working class. Through her writing and eventually, through her public addresses, she encouraged workers to reclaim their power and take ownership of the tools they worked with to earn their daily bread.

Lucy was known to have controversial views on race, gender, and politics. She was perceived as being unexpectedly rough around the edges when expressing her views despite having the appearance of a classy Victorian woman of the time. In her speeches, she openly expressed how she'd like to witness the public deaths of the wealthy elite pioneering capitalism under the guise of democracy. These lectures made Lucy more enigmatic and allowed her to grab the attention of the ears she wanted to twist with her views.

The question of Lucy's race and heritage was controversial. She described herself as a "Spanish-Indian maiden" (Jacob, 2017). She deliberately cultivated racial ambiguity to point out that your speech and actions are more defining than the race you happen to be born into. She stated, "I am not a candidate for office, and the public have no right to my past. I am battling for a principle" (Hunter, 2018). Lucy did not campaign within African-American communities and received criticism for hiding her race. Despite this, Lucy stood out as a woman of color and this drew attention to her passionate speeches for workers' rights.

May Day!

Lucy used her husband's position as the editor of *The Alarm* to her advantage to spread the word about their radical anarchist ideals. She soon became a member of the Working Women's Union in Chicago, where she took an active role in organizing labor meetings, strikes, and public forums. Lucy wielded her pen like a sword throughout her career as a journalist to challenge the status quo. Socialism called for an equal distribution of wealth and resources, with the greater good being the primary concern of society. Lucy's anarchist views took this ideology to another extreme by calling for the dissolution of the government so that the people could rule themselves in the truest form of democracy.

Albert and Lucy put their written words into action when they emerged as leaders in Chicago's labor organization scene in the 1880s. Albert was a fierce advocate for an eight-hour workday for the working class, and many people supported his demands of the rich capitalist employers profiting from exploiting the working class. The couple took their campaign to the streets of Chicago in the first-ever May Day Parade on 1 May 1886. An astounding 80,000 workers lined the streets of the Windy City and went on strike to protest for shorter working days. At its essence, the strike was a direct attack on capitalism as a system that relied on the blood, sweat, and tears of the working class to stay afloat without letting them benefit from it.

Lucy was at Albert's side, sparking flames within the crowds of workers that gathered to hear their provocative speeches. She called for the blood of the wealthy elite to be shed so the working class could be free from capitalism. The workers of Chicago were frustrated, and they needed support from influential people who spoke up for them. Through her public speaking skills, Lucy earned a reputation as a hypnotic orator whose words went straight to the heart of the working class.

The couple continued to campaign around the city until the events at Haymarket Square, Chicago, on May 4, 1886. The strike ended in the catastrophe of the Haymarket Affair. Lucy and Albert were addressing a group of peaceful protestors at Haymarket Square when a bomb made of dynamite was thrown into the crowd. Police began firing into the crowd, some police officers were included among the fatalities and wounded. The authorities stated that the bomber was an anarchist. Albert was arrested and sent to trial for his alleged involvement in the bombing and incitement of violence among the protesters. In 1892, Albert was executed by the state of Chicago. The grieving Lucy's passion for her cause reached boiling point.

Lucy asserted that the government, mainstream media, and law enforcement were colluding to maintain the imbalanced status quo where the rich become richer, and the poor working class remains downtrodden and ripe for exploitation. She controversially wrote, "Liberty has been named anarchy" (Parsons, 1886). Lucy saw anarchy as the only way to attain freedom from the oppressive economic system smothering American society and politics with its toxic industrial smog. She emphasized that only a certain wealthy few could afford true liberty at the expense of those who could not afford it.

Her work as a journalist became more directly critical of the wealthy entrepreneurs who owned the industries that employed the working class. She continued to travel the country to raise awareness about the lack of fair treatment in labor. Lucy famously wrote, "Bread is freedom and freedom is bread" (Parsons, 1886). This impactful statement encompasses the issues of class politics, gender discrimination, and racism that were plaguing America in the industrial era. Lucy meant that starving people struggle to find the energy to fight for the causes that affect them. The ruling class kept the working class hungry in multiple ways to focus their attention on getting their ration of bread like a carrot being dangled in front of a horse to make it walk. To Lucy, true freedom was worth more than any ration of bread your capitalist employer would "allow" you to have. True freedom meant owning the means to make your own metaphorical bread while those around receive their fair share of the bread.

Lucy's speeches and writing introduced the concept of framing racism and class discrimination as systemic and woven into the fabric of American society. She asserted it could only be eliminated by dissolving the government and allowing the people to rule themselves. The reality was that the homeless, poverty-stricken, overworked, and undereducated working-class families could never keep their heads above water because the government left them drowning in a shallow pool of ignorance while the wealthy elite lined their pockets through exploitation and oppression.

Lucy highlighted the irony of America priding itself on being a nation where freedom and equality were written in stone and practiced in society. In reality, your rights to freedom and equality depended on the color of your skin and your bank balance. The concepts of freedom of speech and assembly were crucial to Lucy yet threatening to the authorities. The Chicago Police Department once described Lucy and her husband as "more dangerous than a thousand rioters" (Gallagher, 2016).

Lucy's Legacy

Lucy campaigned tirelessly for the upliftment of the working class. She fought for them to reclaim their power and leverage their position as the (almost broken) backbone of America's supposedly "free" capitalist economy. Her political activism culminated in her forming the International Workers of the World (IWW) or the "Wobblies" in 1905 in Chicago. The organization acted as a general trade union for workers from various industries. Workers across America united under the banner of the IWW to take direct action against unfair working conditions, working hours, and workplace discrimination. The organization lit up Chicago's workforce by encouraging solidarity across industries. Its aim was mass revolutionary action to challenge the power of the wealthy employers who employed the working class. The organization currently has more than 12,000 members, a testament to Lucy's impact as an activist and revolutionary.

The significance of the May Day Strike of 1886 is still celebrated today on International Workers' Day. It's also known as May Day or Labor Day. The day is a public holiday in many countries as a reminder of the sacrifices made by workforces of the past to help us progress to the extensive workers' rights we're afforded today.

Lucy made her voice heard above the loud capitalist crowd as she fought her way through it. As a woman of color leading influential political campaigns, her statements meant more to the workers than the empty promises given by the white politicians trying to garner support to elevate themselves. Lucy shrugged off the constraints of race and gender to be who she wanted to be; she had a sense of freedom foreign to many women of color at the time.

At the age of 91, Lucy died in a house fire. She was laid to rest near Haymarket Square in Chicago, a place of great significance to Lucy's political and personal life. She is celebrated through monuments, streets, and parks named in her honor. The Lucy Parsons Center in Boston and the Lucy Parsons Labs in Chicago were built as tributes to Lucy's legacy.

Chapter Seven

Clara Lemlich Shavelson

An Incendiary Immigrant in New York

I am a working girl. One of those who are on strike against intolerable conditions. I am tired of listening to speakers who talk in general terms. What we are here for is to decide whether we shall strike or shall not strike.
—Clara Lemlich

The final tale of women who sparked revolutions during the era of industrialization moves us into the Progressive Era to New York City in the early 1900s. The city streets were full of economic and social activity, mostly due to the immigrant families who had made the city their home. Their rich and varied heritage became the needles and thread that wove the colorful fabric of New York City together as a melting pot of cultures. The literal needles, thread, and fabric were what kept the immigrant population employed in factories as the garment industry continued to expand.

The Progressive Era from the 1890s to the 1920s saw significant reforms in the U.S. The struggles relating to workers' rights, the rights of immigrant workers, social welfare, and women's rights came to the fore of American society. It was a period known for mass strikes, political activism, and social progress. The working class used the developments from the past decade to increase their awareness and question the legitimacy of the wealthy elite. The workers challenged corruption, wealth-hoarding, and the mistreatment of employees.

Throughout the Industrial Revolution, there was a steady influx of immigrant workers to America. They arrived on American soil to escape religious or political persecution in their home countries, hoping to improve their lives. Like many Jewish immigrants, Clara Lemlich had fled the brutal pogroms in her homeland of Ukraine. The pogroms were a form of ethnic cleansing practiced in Eastern Europe, in which the Jewish population was either expelled or massacred. Hoping to find peace and safety in America, and despite their key contributions to the boom of the textile and garment industry in New York, the newly-arrived immigrants faced mistreatment and discrimination at work. Clara was a prominent figure in the Strike known as the "Uprising of the 20,000," which is the largest strike of female workers in U.S. history.

Early Life

Clara was born in Eastern Europe in 1886 to a Jewish family. Her hometown of Horodok (sometimes called Gorodok) was originally part of Russia but is now part of western Ukraine. It was a largely rural, patriarchal society, where the father, brothers, or husband was the head of the household. She was excluded from the village school due to antisemitism, but Clara hoarded books and studied Russian, in addition to her native Yiddish, despite her father's strong opposition. Her family fled persecution for the shores of America in 1903 when Clara was 17.

Jewish populations have been persecuted throughout history, and Eastern Europe in the early 20th century was sadly no exception to these brutal crimes against humanity. Clara's family left for America to escape the pogroms of Eastern Europe, where Jews were brutally murdered on a mass scale during riots based on anti-Semitic beliefs. The Jews of Eastern Europe received financial support from the Jewish population in America, and many had the means to move to the U.S. based on aid from these Jewish-American sympathizers.

Throughout her childhood, Clara practiced sewing, writing, and language. Her sewing skills and tenacity allowed her to find a job in the growing garment businesses of New York City. Clara soon became a fabric draper for garment shops to help support her family. It was here

Clara would earn her reputation as a firestarter for improvements for textile factory workers, garment workers, and women. Her roots in socialism had been laid when Clara was a teenager back home in Horodok. A friend introduced her to socialist ideology by exposing her to the writings of socialist revolutionaries who believed that the only way the working class could survive was to overthrow the wealthy elite, take ownership of the means of production, and distribute wealth for the greater good.

A Firebrand in the Factory

As a child, Clara was known to be defiant of gender stereotypes and social norms through her actions. She chose to educate herself through voracious reading, taking care to hide her Russian books from her father, who saw it as the language of the oppressors. Growing up as a Jew in Ukraine, Clara had experienced discrimination from a young age and was familiar with its every nuance. She had adopted socialist ideologies before even landing in America and was a firm believer in working for the greater good of her community. Her arrival in New York City exposed her to the harsh realities of urban life, class politics, social hierarchy, and economic discrimination based on her ethnicity and faith.

> "The older, skilled male workers who dominated the union resisted her efforts, but whenever they attempted to strike with-

out informing the women, Clara brazenly warned them that their union would never get off the ground until they made an effort to include women. Over the men's objections, she brought her women coworkers out on strike again and again in various garment shops between 1907 and 1909" (Orleck, 1999).

Before the Triangle Shirtwaist Strike in 1909, Clara actively mobilized groups of female workers to go on strike and boycott local businesses to create awareness of the conditions garment workers were subjected to.

Clara was known to be generous amongst her colleagues, a good singer, and a natural leader. "The most famous of the farbrente Yidishe *meydlekh*, meaning "fiery Jewish girls," whose militancy helped to galvanize the labor movement" (Orleck, 1999). Clara's bravery would be tested in 1909 when the working conditions at the garment businesses and textile factories of New York caused tensions to reach boiling point.

Uprising of the 20,000

New York was the leading producer of high-quality garments in 1909, and the women's blouse or shirtwaist was one of the most widely used items of clothing. The fashion industry had progressed from handmade clothing made in people's homes to mass-produced clothing made in factories and available to buy in garment shops. The manufacturing of clothing on this large scale was commonly known as the "needle trades." In the early 1900s, the shirtwaist industry in New York numbered close to 32,000 workers, and it was one of the most structured industries in all of America, earning a total of $50 million in 1909 alone. Most of these workers were women who were [also] immigrants from Italy, Russia, Poland, and Ireland.

The employees in the shirtwaist factories were organized and paid according to their skill set. Machine operators earned about $4 a week at most, and designers and sample cutters earned up to $20 a week. The higher-earning employees were mostly male, while the lower-income employees were mostly female. This was outright discrimination based on gender, and the gender pay gap was considerable. The male employees often bullied and even sexually harassed female employees because the attitude within the factories was that the female workforce was dispensable and easily replaceable. Women like Clara had led strikes against these oppressive gender stereotypes, and the women had to face even more dismissive attitudes in the factories in an attempt to keep them quiet.

In 1909, the employees of the Triangle Shirtwaist Factory and Leiserson Company, two of the largest shirtwaist suppliers in New York, took to the streets in protest of the working conditions at the factories. They were protesting the fact that their workload was unreasonable. They only earned $2 a day and were fined if they made a mistake with stitching the fabric. They had to bring in their sewing machines and sew mass amounts of garments before the end of the workday. Workers also had to pay for the needles and thread used to sew the fabric together. They worked 14-hour days and were only allowed one break during the day. The denial of bathroom breaks led to workers urinating on the factory floor in desperation. The conditions were made even more inhumane by insufficient ventilation due to locked factory doors. "In June of 1909, a fire prevention specialist sent a letter to the owners of the Triangle Shirtwaist Factory to discuss ways to improve safety in the factory. This letter was ignored" (Boehm, 2013). This unheeded warning would lead to tragedy, as we will see in the next chapter.

The strikers were predominantly female, and they were angry. They wanted freedom from their oppressors, privacy at work, better pay, promotion opportunities, shorter working hours, and safer working conditions. The company directors refused to listen to the workers, so tensions continued to build. Clara was seen as a troublemaker during the initial strikes leading up to the Triangle Shirtwaist Factory Strike, even by the ILGWU, a women's trade union led by men. She was arrested 17 times by the police sent in to use brutality to break up the strikers. Clara was also severely beaten by thugs that were hired by the company directors to threaten the workers into submission.

The true revolution began on November 22, 1909, when a meeting was held to gather the shirtwaist factory workers to strategize. The majority of these workers were young women who could barely speak English and were afraid of losing their jobs. Clara, with a few broken ribs and bruises, listened to men who were leaders of the various unions drone on for two hours about what the workers needed to do to prepare for the strike. Clara was frustrated and disappointed in their lack of fighting spirit. She stood up and demanded the crowd's attention. Speaking in her native language of Yiddish, the 23-year-old fiercely and confidently addressed the crowd of distressed workers. Clara made her way to the front of the meeting hall and said, "I have listened to all the speakers, and I have no further patience for talk. I am one who feels and suffers from the things pictured. I move we go on strike" (Schofield, 1984).

Despite her six broken ribs, Clara joined the 20,000 young women on the streets of New York and demanded change. Almost 70% of the strikers were female, and 90% were Jewish (Michels, 1999). As in the case of the Match Workers Strike in London, it took women of higher social standing to generate interest from the press. "Ann Morgan, daughter of international financier JP Morgan, took up the cause of the striking workers. Joining her in support of the workers was Alva Vanderbilt Belmont" (Boehm, 2013). These rich women, also known as the "mink brigade," brought publicity to the strike.

The strike lasted 11 weeks and brought New York's garment production to a halt. Many factory owners approached the trade unions to reach a truce so they could get their machines whirring again. The Triangle Shirtwaist Factory owners Max Blanck and Isaac Harris employed dirty tactics such as hiring prostitutes and ex-prize fighters to fight with the picketers. "Bribed policemen arrested any who fought back and dragged them off to court bandaged and bloodied. Bribed judges found workers guilty" (Boehm, 2013). The strike ended abruptly in February of 1910, with the factory owners agreeing to better pay and working conditions but not to union representation. Many workers returned to their jobs out of fear.

Clara's passionate call to action set the wheels in motion to change the way the shirtwaist factories of New York treated their employees. Casual employment fell away for the most part, with many employees signing contracts that set out their employment terms. The work week decreased from about 60 hours to 52 hours, and employees were given formal paid leave days. Importantly, sewing machines and other work equipment were now paid for by the company, and discrimination based on union membership wasn't allowed. Membership numbers of the ILGWU sky-rocketed after the strike and led to the needle trades becoming a beacon of hope for employee rights throughout the country.

Clara's Legacy

Clara's ideals and her call to action were inherently feminist and anti-capitalist. She directly challenged the wealthy male elite by inciting her colleagues to stand with her and demand their employers acknowledge their worth to the needle trades. She addressed the crowd in Yiddish, rousing their pride in their Jewish race. Many young women that worked with Clara were inspired by her bold actions, and the shirtwaist workers developed a sense of community as a result of the partial success of the strike.

Clara's reputation for inciting workers to demand improvements, led to her being blacklisted from the garment industry after the strike. She then shifted her focus to large-scale campaigns to get women the right to vote, and established the Wage Earner's Suffrage League, a nod to her awareness that working-class employees were treated as less important than their middle-class colleagues.

Clara continued to organize and mobilize strikes and boycotts. She encouraged tenants in her area to engage in rent strikes when the local landlords began charging exorbitant rents that most couldn't afford. She led a motion to boycott kosher butcheries that were price-gouging their loyal and local customers. As members of the Communist party, her family was under surveillance and summoned to Washington to testify before the House Committee on Un-American Activities. She was denied a pension from the ILGWU when she retired. Ever the radical, she continued to urge the working class to reclaim their power.

Demonstrating fighting power until the end of her life, Clara convinced the caretakers at her retirement home to form a union to protect their rights. She remained a labor organizer and staunch unionist right until her death in 1982 at the age of 96. Sadly, the workers' demands in the Triangle Shirtwaist strike were barely met. This fateful decision by the company directors to ignore the workers' concerns leads us to the life story of our final fiery female. Rose Schneiderman was Clara's colleague and associate. Her story is wrapped up in the flames of the Triangle Shirtwaist Factory Fire of 1911.

Chapter Eight

ROSE SCHNEIDERMAN

The Red Rose of Anarchy

What the woman who labors wants is the right to live, not simply exist — the right to life as the rich woman has the right to life, and the sun and music and art. You have nothing that the humblest worker has not a right to have also. The worker must have bread, but she must have roses, too. Help, you women of privilege, give her the ballot to fight with. —Rose Schneiderman

The aftermath of the Triangle Shirtwaist Factory Strike of March 1909 resulted in major positive reforms for workers in the rigid and tough garment industry. Because of the actions of labor organizers like Clara Lemlich, workers now had signed contracts that outlined their working hours, leave days, employee rights, and the obligation of their employer to respect these rights. The strike was a watershed moment during the post-industrial Progressive Era because more than 20,000 workers took to the streets as one collective hive of awareness to fight for their rights. One of these workers, and a key figure in organizing the strike, was Polish immigrant Rose Schneiderman.

Despite the progression towards modernization and away from the sweatshop mentality, the directors of the Triangle Shirtwaist Company refused to heed their employees' cries. This ignorance proved fatal when the Triangle Company's factory in Washington Square caught alight and claimed the lives of many workers. An actual fire had been sparked by the employer's ignorance of the labor revolution happening within their factory walls. Rose was one of the many devastated and traumatized by the carnage of the fire for the female workforce. She used the tragedy as an opportunity to pressurize the greedy capitalists into progress through campaigning for safer working conditions.

Early Life

Rose was born in 1882 in a small village in Poland. Her family was dedicated to their Jewish faith, and they made Rose's education about their faith and the world their highest priority. It was uncommon and even frowned upon by rural communities to educate a daughter. Nevertheless, Rose's parents uprooted the family home so she could attend school to learn Hebrew and become literate. This bold move would serve Rose well in her career as a labor activist. Rose's parents were both highly skilled in the needle trades, and her mother was a master seamstress. Rose was already on a trajectory to join the garment industry, and this path was cemented when the Schneidermans decided to move to New York in 1890.

They settled in the Lower East Side and did their best to find work in the burgeoning fashion industry. Tragedy struck the hopeful family in 1892 when Rose's father, unfortunately, passed away, leaving the Schneidermans without their breadwinner. Rose's mother tried her best to make ends meet, and she wanted to make sure Rose had better opportunities than herself. She wanted Rose to have a respectable job and this meant staying out of the factory system. Rose tried to work as a salesperson for the many garment shops lining the streets of New York City. However, financially, this "pink-collar" job paid a lot less than the blue-collar (but less respectable) job of working on the textile factory floor.

Mrs. Schneiderman's hopes for Rose to abandon the limitations of being a working-class woman were further dashed when she had to abandon her children at an orphanage when Rose was just 13 years old. The family separated because of the struggles that came with urbanization and being an immigrant. It was sadly common for immigrant families to split apart even though they came to America to escape and for a second chance at success. Rose had to drop out of school and focus on earning a living.

However, before becoming a reluctant cog in the industrial capitalist machine, Rose lived in Montreal, Canada, for a short period. This brief stay had a profound impact on Rose's career as a political activist. She was introduced to the concept of labor movements, trade unions, the impact of strikes, and ideologies that were considered radical, like socialism and communism.

In 1903, when she was 21, Rose moved back to New York to start her career as a factory worker. She started out by making hats and caps in a factory, and just like Clara, Rose couldn't accept the gender pay gap and the fact that men were given better-paying jobs, regardless of their skills. Her first act of labor organizing was venting her frustration by recruiting 25 fellow cap makers to officially join the United Cloth Hat and Cap Makers Union. The stage was set for Rose to fan the flames of revolution from inside the belly of the industrial beast.

The Triangle Shirtwaist Factory Fire

Rose was tiny in stature, but her head of flaming red hair might have acted as a warning to those who doubted her power as a revolutionary! As a cap maker, she soon began to organize strikes and walk-outs while demanding better working conditions and higher wages. Those in power saw her challenges to authority as trouble, but she persevered regardless of the obstacles in her way. By the age of 26, in 1908, Rose was elected as the vice president of the New York branch of the Women's Trade Union League

(WTUL). Rose decided early on to leave her post at the factory to become a full-time employee of the WTUL. It showed dedication to her cause because this was a risky move. Work was hard to come by, and the cost of living was high. She would go on to have an illustrious career with the League, serving as the union's national president from 1926 to 1950. Through her high-ranking position, Rose was able to transform the labor landscape by making New York a hub for labor reform and progress.

Rose's focus during her trade union organization was on class politics, especially between different classes of women. She had first-hand experience of the struggles of losing her femininity and being exposed to life's worst hardships as a working-class woman. She juxtaposed their experiences against those of the upper-class women around them to highlight the unfairness and discrimination workers faced, even though they were all women. Her speech relating to the concept of "Bread and Roses" delved deeper into this and will be discussed in the coming paragraphs. Rose became known amongst the workers as a powerful orator whose words reached the heart of the issues faced by the working class in a brutal yet poetic way.

Rose took an active role in the Triangle Shirtwaist Factory Strike of 1909 alongside Clara and the other trade unionists. Rose and Clara were both radical in their views and determined in their actions. They used their gift of articulating the struggles of the people who had no voice to rouse their colleagues' spirits and demand attention to their cause. A major issue the protestors wanted to address during the 1909 Strike was the lack of ventilation and fire safety in the textile factories. It was frighteningly common for a factory's fire exits to be sealed up or access to them restricted because of the employers' paranoia that materials might be stolen or that workers might take unsanctioned breaks. Fire escapes were often nothing more than narrow stairwells, and barely complied with city codes. Add to this that the workers were working with flammable materials like cotton and lint. The lack of occupational health and safety amounted to another form of oppression against the working class. Their employers viewed them as desperate criminals undeserving of basic human decency through safety.

There had been factory fires in other states, like New Jersey, where workers had died leading up to that fateful Saturday afternoon of the Triangle Shirtwaist Factory Fire. Rose and the other WTUL members campaigned for improved safety by addressing large crowds of mostly female workers. She criticized the factory owners for abusing legal loopholes and the lack of city fire department inspections to avoid implementing meaningful fire safety precautions. The Triangle Company was a particular target of Rose's wrath in her speeches because they were the largest shirtwaist manufacturer in the market and the only company that refused to adopt the labor reforms taking over other factories in the city.

Triangle's factory in Washington Square was set up like a sweatshop. The building was 10 stories high, and the work desks were arranged in a maze-like pattern so the owners could pack in as many workers as possible to maximize production. They violated the maximum number of workers allowed in a space per cubic meter of air. The fire escapes were either sealed shut or so narrow that only one person at a time could squeeze through to access the stairwells. Despite being well aware of other recent factory fires, the scathing rhetoric of activists like Rose, and the risks they were exposing their workers to, the Triangle Company did nothing to improve factory safety.

On that fateful Saturday afternoon of 25 March 1911, a cigarette was accidentally thrown onto the scraps of fabric left lying around on the eighth floor. It was common practice for this scrap fabric to be piled high under every sewing table in the factory. It created the perfect path for the fire to rapidly rage right up to the 10th floor. The material caught alight, and the fire spread in a matter of minutes. Workers who saw the flames early managed to squeeze into the fire escape stairwells and exit the building in time. Logically, the other workers still inside reached for the factory's firehose, but the hose was so rusty that it wouldn't open. The elevators didn't work fast enough to get enough workers to safety. The whole factory was engulfed in angry flames within 20 minutes, trapping the workers on the ninth and tenth floors. The fire department arrived quickly, but their ladder only reached up to the sixth floor of the Triangle building.

The fire claimed the lives of 146 Triangle Shirtwaist Factory workers. Some were burned alive while trying to squeeze through the narrow stairwells and doorways, others burned while waiting for the elevator to take them to safety, and 62 women perished by jumping out of the factory windows from the ninth floor. Most of the young women were Jewish and Italian immigrant workers. The fire was easily preventable, and the conditions inside the factory were a tinderbox waiting to be lit. The rapid spread of the fire provided a play-by-play account of the glaringly obvious safety risks the employees were exposed to daily.

Bread and Roses

All the strikes we have examined thus far protested labor conditions that threatened women's health and lives. They all acted as clear warnings that an event like the Triangle Shirtwaist Factory Fire was inevitable. The individual accidents resulting from the dangers in the mills and factories had not led to significant reform. This fire was the result of decades of unheeded warnings and did finally result in mass protest, outrage, and reform. The fire at the Triangle factory traumatized almost 40,000 textile factory workers in New York. The negligence and uncaring actions and omissions of the company's directors were now glaringly obvious. The city could no longer deny that the factory owners were exploiting workers for profit at the literal expense of workers' lives. The directors were charged with manslaughter for their negligence in failing to improve safety at the factory. However, it would still be decades before occupational health and safety precautions became a basic legal requirement for companies to comply with.

The trial ended with the directors being acquitted of the charges.

Rose was one of the many WTUL leaders who were enraged by the incident because it could have been prevented, and lives could have been saved. She once again took to the streets of New York to tackle the problem in the way she had become known for. Less than two weeks after the fire in April 1911, when the trauma was fresh, Rose addressed her WTUL colleagues about the aftermath. She spoke about the harsh realities of being a factory worker and the callousness with which the companies treated them. She emphasized that their struggles as women were different from those of their male colleagues. From this angle, Rose made her famous remarks about "bread and roses." She pointed out that "the woman worker needs bread, but she needs roses too" (Orleck, 1999). The bread represented meeting their basic needs as humans, like a living wage, reasonable workloads, work days that were less than 14 hours, and safe working conditions. Roses were the femininities that had eluded so many young women when they joined the factory system. These were things they needed to progress from just surviving to thriving. "Roses" included intellectual stimulation, socializing with like-minded women, learning from each other, and enjoying their lives as fulfilled individuals.

Rose was a powerful orator. She addressed the audience at a memorial meeting held in the Metropolitan Opera House on April 2, 1911:

> This is not the first time girls have been burned alive in the city. Every week I must learn of the untimely death of one of my sister workers. Every year thousands of us are maimed...Public officials have only words of warning to us... and they have the workhouse just back of all their warnings. The strong hand of the law beats us back, when we rise, into the conditions that make life unbearable. It is up to the working people to save themselves (New York Survey Associates et al., 1911/2007).

Rose brought the underlying class and gender politics at play in the factory system to the surface. She used her high profile and platform to criticize the wealthy women of the upper classes for believing they were "doing their bit" to help the working-class women by making vapid donations to fickle charity organizations. She encouraged all women to speak out against the brutality of the sweatshop conditions that factory workers were subjected to and the dangerous machinery they were forced to work with. The deaths of the mostly female workers at the Triangle Shirtwaist Factory painted a real picture of how urgently the underlying issues need to be called out and addressed. Instead of perceiving the fire one-dimensionally as a tragedy, Rose repositioned it as a means for legal reform of safety in an industrial workplace. Taking swift action, Rose worked with Clara and other female trade unionists to form the

Wage Earner's Suffrage League in 1911. It was an organization focused on the plight of working-class employees.

Rose's Legacy

Rose's powerful words and her actions provided fuel to help spread the fires of change across the factories of New York City. Out of the flames of tragedy came definite improvement. The lives of poor immigrant workers, mostly Jewish and Italian, were uplifted and made safer thanks to the newly implemented workplace safety standards. Rose paved the way for concepts like occupational health and safety and compensation for work-related injuries to become the norm for every business. She contributed to workers having a legal right to sue an employer for failing to create a safe working environment.

The impact Rose left on concrete legislative changes still stands up to today. She was actively involved in drafting the Fair Labor Standards Act and the Social Security Act during President Roosevelt's time in office in the 1930s. She pioneered many reforms as part of his New Deal government program in the wake of the Great Depression. Her positive impact in the legislature coincided with her close relationship with the Roosevelts, especially the first lady, Eleanor Roosevelt. The influential couple believed in Rose's ideas for labor reform and provided her with a platform to realize them, to the benefit of all workers. Rose was fiercely proud of her Jewish culture, religion, and heritage. She used this pride to campaign for the freedom of Jewish prisoners in Nazi-occupied Europe during World War II.

Rose's experiences as a factory worker and her socialist ideals motivated her to dedicate her life to fighting for the rights of workers and women. She was adamant that women should have the right to vote because they are human. She was frustrated by the fact women were expected to work and contribute to the country's economy but were not allowed to be involved in making decisions that greatly affected their daily lives. Her analogy of "bread and roses" in relation to women's rights has been used by many labor activists after her and continues to ring true today. Like so many other campaigners, Rose was also a suffragist, fighting hard for the women's ballot as the only legitimate way to ensure long-term equality. Rose never married but had a long-term relationship with fellow labor movement colleague Maud Swartz, her travel and work partner, whom she described as "a wonderful companion" (Orleck, 1995). Rose passed away at the age of 90 in New York, the city she had dedicated her life to reforming.

Chapter Nine

CONCLUSION

Women that believe in each other can survive anything. Women who believe in each other create armies that will win kingdoms and wars. —Nikita Gill

We've reached the end of our journey through the stories of bravery and determination of the fiery females we've met along the way. Your journey of discovery in learning about these brave women might be at an end, but the fight to end gender discrimination and unfair treatment of workers is far from over. The female workforce of today still faces an enormous amount of prejudice, lack of recognition, harassment, and misogyny. Their voices are still silenced, regardless of their qualifications or status in society. The gender pay gap is a real issue impacting women's ability to take care of themselves and their families, especially where they are the head of the household. Let's recap the lessons we've learned from the women who sparked a revolution for their colleagues and the women of future generations.

We've traveled back and forth across the Atlantic, between the industrialized nations of Britain and the U.S., across almost a century (1836-1911) on our adventure to meet the revolutionary women who fanned the flames of change in the industries they worked in. These women endured abuse, injustice, unfairness, and discrimination based on their gender and, for some, also on their race. They took a brave stand and decided to take action to change how they were being treated, a cause many of them were willing to sacrifice their lives for. A common thread between all the women we've profiled is that they were passionate anti-capitalists. They were all radicalized against the system in place through learning about socialism and communism. They dedicated their lives to an equal distribution of wealth and human rights for the greater good of society.

What makes their actions even more outstanding is that they spoke up during a time when women could barely own the clothes on their backs or say a word in public, let alone publicly protest against injustice. Our fiery females defied and sometimes even mocked the gender stereotypes they were expected to conform to. These included the expectation of them to be the timid victims that the media and literary works of the time portrayed them to be. They were expected to accept being treated as inferior to men and exist without basic human rights. The women we met during the brutal working days of the Industrial Revolution refused to accept the status quo. These women rejected the idea that the most vulnerable in society, which included women and children who were often poor, uneducated, and from immigrant families or African-American, were allowed to be exploited by the powerful white male capitalist leaders of the industry.

The actions and impact of the women who sparked a revolution can be divided into two distinct categories: the narrators and the mobilizers. The narrators include Harriet Hanson Robinson from Lowell, Annie Besant from London, Lucy Parsons from Virginia, and Rose Schneiderman from New York. These women wielded their pens like swords and words like shields, campaigning tirelessly for workers' and women's rights throughout their lives. They had the advantage of intellect to write down the oppression they watched being doled out on the working class by the capitalist industrial factory owners. They formed their observations, interpretations, comparisons, and analogies in such a way that roused the spirits of the working class, and incited them to take action. Their bird's eye view of where the tensions were building allowed them to steer the fight for fairness in the direction that would create the most impact. Their articles and speeches were cynical yet sincere, harsh yet vulnerable, and complicated yet poetic in their simplicity. What made these narrators so influential was their understanding of how to remove the teeth of class politics while working in the belly of the beast, which was the factory floor. These story-tellers gave the female workforce and workers, in general, a voice that was either silenced or nonexistent during the Industrial Era. It's through them that the stories and impacts of these strikes live on and continue to inspire. The greatest stories exist whether or not they're told, but the way they're told can change the world.

The mobilizers include Sarah Bagley from Lowell, Sarah Chapman from London, the washerwomen from Atlanta (Dora Jones, Matilda Crawford, Sarah Collier, Sallie Bell, Orphelia Turner, and Carrie Jones), and Clara Lemlich Shavelson from New York. These women took direct action and metaphorically "got their hands dirty" by standing on soap boxes in their workspaces and encouraging their colleagues to bravely walk out. They used their natural leadership skills to influence those around them to see the unfairness the narrators were furiously writing about. None of these women could foresee the impact of the collective strike actions they organized, but they still chose to push forward. They were part of the abusive factory systems they vowed to protest against, and this gave them a unique perspective to inspire other workers to join them. These formidable women ignited the sparks that caused thousands of workers to know their worth and walk out until they were treated better.

The narrators and mobilizers were equally important and necessary to fuel the fires of revolution during the Industrial Revolution and the Progressive Era. Their actions, beliefs, and words changed the world for the working class and women. Let's take courage from the examples of the women profiled in these stories, to speak out for equal rights and fair working conditions. We can no doubt be inspired by these exceptional women's tales of courage in the face of oppression by the leaders of industry, the church, and the state. Ask yourself which fiery female and which story inspires you the most. You might be drawn to the sense of community developed by the women in the mills of Lowell, astounded by the scale of organization of the strike at the Bryant & May Match Factory, feel inspired by the grassroots activism amongst the laundresses of Atlanta, or admire the occupational large-scale health and safety reform brought about by strike at the Triangle Shirtwaist Factory. These stories are a testament to the fact that your value as a human matters more than your status, class, heritage, race, ethnicity, or gender. These women were trailblazers because they fought for their right to be treated with human decency and to be afforded the opportunities to exercise their human rights. The potential to follow in their footsteps and become a trailblazer exists within every woman and young girl because women's rights are human rights.

If you have enjoyed the reading ***Blazing the Way***, it would be greatly appreciated if you would be so kind as to leave a review on Amazon. Credit is due to you as a reader for having the curiosity to want to explore this subject and help restore the stories of women who have often been left behind and forgotten by, or written out of, history. Reviews make all the difference to independent authors. Scanning the QR code below will take you to the 'leave a review' area of the book. Thank you!

ABOUT THE AUTHOR

Elise Baker has a lifelong interest in women's history and feminism. Her passion is excavating the past to unearth the stories of women whose remarkable feats and accomplishments have been buried and forgotten because of their gender in the hope that they can fuel and inspire women of today to face adversity and discrimination with courage. In learning about the achievements of these remarkable women, we address the serious shortage of women in the historical accounts of the Industrial Revolution. Women labor leaders contributed to the progress of women within the workforce, regardless of who knew about it. They all knew their efforts would likely go unrecognized, yet they put their lives on the line regardless. Their stories offer a balanced perspective on the evolution of labor rights. May they serve as inspiration to women to continue making a difference and occupying important spaces.

Elise's maternal family, from the borderlands of the Czech Republic, became refugees with no country to belong to after the Second World War and dispersed all over the world. She grew up listening to her grandmother's recollections of this time, and believes that understanding and learning from the bravery of ordinary women is essential in shaping the future. She holds an Honors degree and a Postgraduate Diploma that led to a career as a librarian, archivist, and eventually an editor for television. She loves traveling to different countries and experiencing different cultures. When she's not reading or writing, she enjoys walking with her dog along the beach and seeing plays at the theater with family and friends.

ALSO BY

To keep an eye out for new titles, bringing more forgotten stories of women's achievements to light, and to sign up for Elise Baker's monthly newsletter please visit: www.elise-baker.com

Women Code Breakers: The Best Kept Secret of WWII *True Stories of Female Code Breakers Whose Top-Secret Work Helped Win World War II*

Princess, Countess, Socialite, Spy: *True Stories of High-Society Ladies Turned WWII Spies*

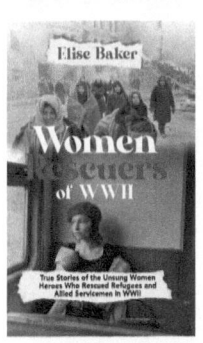
Women Rescuers of WWII: *True Stories of Unsung Women Heroes Who Rescued Refugees and Allied Servicemen in WWII*

Nightingales, Bluebirds and Angels of Mercy: *True Stories of the Courage and Heroism of Nurses on the Front Line in WWII*

REFERENCES & BIBLIOGRAPHY

AFL-CIO. (n.d.). *Atlanta's Washerwomen Strike.* AFL-CIO. Retrieved March 29, 2023, from https://aflcio.org/about/history/labor-history-events/atlanta-washer-women-strike

Aitken, R., & Aitken, M. (2010). *The Triangle Fire: Tragedy, Trial, and Triumph. Litigation, 36*(3), 53–56. https://www.jstor.org/stable/29760788

Amplify.(2023, November 26). *The Women of the Atlanta Washerwomen Strike of 1881.*HerStry. https://herstryblg.com/amplify/2020/11/2/amplify-the-women-of-the-atlanta-washerwomen-strike-of-1881

Argesinger, J A E. (2016b). *The Triangle Fire With Documents* Bedford/St Martin's

AZ Quotes. (n.d.-a). *Quotes by Harriet Hanson Robinson.* AZ Quotes. Retrieved March 29, 2023, from https://www.azquotes.com/author/54313-Harriet_Hanson_Robinson

AZ Quotes. (n.d.-b). *Top 16 Quotes by Rose Schneiderman.* AZ Quotes. Retrieved March 29, 2023, from https://www.azquotes.com/author/41523-Rose_Schneiderman

AZ Quotes. (n.d.-c). *Top 25 Quotes by Annie Besant.*
AZ Quotes. Retrieved March 29, 2023, from https://www.azquotes.com/author/1340-Annie_Besant

Banerjee, A., & Johnson, C. (2020, February 26).
African American Workers Built America. Clasp. https://www.clasp.org/blog/african-american-workers-built-america/

Bender, D.E. (2004b). *Sweated Work, Weak Bodies: Anti-Sweatshop Campaigns and Languages of Labor* Rutgers University Press

Black Past. (2007, January 28). (*1886)*
Lucy Parsons, "I am An Anarchist." Black Past.

Blake, W. (1804). And Did Those Feet in Ancient Time. *Poetry Foundation*. Retrieved April 3, 2023, from https://www.poetryfoundation.org/poems/54684/jerusalem-and-did-those-feet-in-ancient-time

Bloom, M. (2017, May 1). *Chicago Woman Who Led 1st May Day Parade In 1886 Honored With Street Sign.*
DNA Info. https://www.dnainfo.com/chicago/20170501/avondale/lucy-gonzalez-parsons-street-sign-avondale-may-day-1886-labor-organizer/

Boehm, A. (2013, March 9). *Triangle Shirtwaist Factory women strike, win better wages and hours, New York, 1909.*
Global Nonviolent Action Database.
https://nvdatabase.swarthmore.edu/content/triangle-shirtwaist-factory-women-strike-win-better-wages-and-hours-new-york-1909

Brain, J. (2021, April 19). The Match Girls Strike. Historic UK.
https://www.historic-uk.com/HistoryUK/HistoryofBritain/Match-Girls-Strike/

Carson, J. (2021b) *A Matter of Moral Justice: Black Women Laundry Workers and the Fight for Justice. (Working Class in American History)* Illinois University Press

Casey, C. G. (2010). *Lowell Mill Girls* [Youtube video]. https://www.youtube.com/watch?v=pkJwOYagvuI&ab_channel=ColleenGCasey

Cohn, S. B. (2017). *Clara Lemlich Shavelson: An Activist Life* [Masters Thesis]. https://academicworks.cuny.edu/cgi/viewcontent.cgi

Coser, R.L, Anker, L. J., Penn, A. (1999b). *Women of Courage: Jewish and Italian Immigrant Women in New York.* Praeger

Dickens, C. (1852). One of the Evils of Match-making. *Household Words, V,* 152–155. Dickens Journals Online. https://www.djo.org.uk/household-words/volume-v/page-155.html

Dublin, T. (1975). Women, Work, and the Family: Female Operatives in the Lowell Mills, 1830-1860. *Feminist Studies, 3*(1/2), 30. https://doi.org/10.2307/3518953

Dublin, T. (1979). *Women at work: the transformation of work and community in Lowell, Massachusetts, 1826-1860.* Columbia University Press.

Dublin, T. (2012, August 3). *Women and the Early Industrial Revolution in the United States.* Gilder Lehrman Institute of American History. https://ap.gilderlehrman.org/essay/women-and-early-industrial-revolution-united-states

Dwyer, J. (2011, March 23). *About New York; One Woman Who Changed The Rules.* The New York Times. https://archive.nytimes.com/query.nytimes.com/gst/fullpage-9807E0D91231F930A15750C0A9679D8B63.html

East End Women's Museum. (2016, July 19). *Mary Driscoll: Matchwoman, strike leader and shop owner. East End Women's Museum.* https://eastendwomensmuseum.org/blog/mary-driscoll-matchwoman-strike-leader-and-shop-owner

English Heritage. (n.d.-a). *Annie Besant | Social Reformer | Blue Plaques.* English Heritage. Retrieved March 29, 2023, from https://www.english-heritage.org.uk/visit/blue-plaques/annie-besant/

English Heritage. (n.d.-b). *Match Girls' Strike | Bryant and May works | Blue Plaques*. English Heritage. Retrieved March 29, 2023, from https://www.english-heritage.org.uk/visit/blue-plaques/match-girls-strike/

Francis, C. (2018). *From a Spark to a Blaze: The Matchgirls Strike of 1888*. Marx Talks. https://www.marxtalks.com.au/talk/from-a-spark-to-a-blaze-the-matchgirls-strike-of-1888

Gallagher, K. (2016, November 15). *More Dangerous Than a Thousand Rioters: The Revolutionary Life of Lucy Parsons*. The Nation. https://www.thenation.com/article/archive/more-dangerous-than-a-thousand-rioters-the-revolutionary-life-of-lucy-parsons/

Giaimo, C. (2017, March 8). *Remembering Sarah Bagley, the Voice of America's First Women's Labor Movement*. Atlas Obscura. https://www.atlasobscura.com/articles/lowell-mill-girls-sarah-bagley-strike

Goodman, E. (2023, March 8). *20 Confidence-Boosting Quotes from Seriously Awesome Women in History*. Reader's Digest. https://www.rd.com/list/womens-history-quotes/

Greenberg, Z. (2018, August 1). *Overlooked No More: Clara Lemlich Shavelson, Crusading Leader of Labor Rights*. The New York Times. https://www.nytimes.com/2018/08/01/obituaries/overlooked-clara-lemlich-shavelson.html

Greenwald, R. A. (2002). "The Burning Building at 23 Washington Place": The Triangle Fire, Workers and Reformers in Progressive Era New York. *New York History, 83*(1), 55–91. https://www.jstor.org/stable/23183517

Guy-Sheftall, B. (1992). Black Women's Studies: The Interface of Women's Studies and Black Studies. *Phylon (1960), 49*(1/2), 33–41. https://doi.org/10.2307/3132615

Halsal, P. (1997). *Internet History Sourcebooks.* Fordham. https://sourceboo
ks.fordham.edu/mod/robinson-lowell.asp

Hanson Robinson, H. J. (1898). *Loom and spindle: or, Life among the early
mill girls: with a sketch of "The Lowell offering" and some of its contributors.*

Helmbold, L. R., & Schofield, A. (1989). Women's Labor History,
1790-1945. *Reviews in American History, 17*(4), 501. https://doi.org/1
0.2307/2703424

History Extra. (2021, October 27). The 1888 Matchgirls strike: how a group
of East End women changed British labour history. *History Extra.*
https://www.historyextra.com/period/victorian/match-girls-strike-1888
-east-end-victorian-women-cause/

Hunter, T. W. (1999a). African-American Women Workers' Protest in the
New South. *OAH Magazine of History, 13*(4), 52–55. https://www.jst
or.org/stable/25163311

Hunter, T. W. (1999b). *To 'joy my freedom : Southern Black women's lives and
labors after the Civil War.* Cambridge Harvard University Press.

Hunter, T. W. (2018, January 12). Review | Latina heroine or black radical?
The complicated story of Lucy Parsons. *Washington Post.*
https://www.washingtonpost.com/outlook/latina-heroine-or-black-radic
al-the-complicated-story-of-lucy-parsons/2018/01/10/2126da90-dead-1
1e7-8679-a9728984779c_story.html

Hurt, E. (2023, February 14). *Atlanta's Black history:
The 1881 washerwomen strike.* Axios.
https://www.axios.com/local/atlanta/2023/02/14/atlanta-washerwomen
-strike-black-history

Husband, J. (1999). "The White Slave of the North": Lowell Mill Women and
the Reproduction of "Free" Labor. *Legacy, 16*(1), 11–21.
https://www.jstor.org/stable/25679285

Jacob, M. (2017, November 15). *Lucy Parsons bio reveals new facts about the birth, ethnicity of the "Goddess of Anarchy."* Chicago Tribune. https://www.chicagotribune.com/entertainment/books/ct-books-lucy-parsons-goddess-of-anarchy-jacqueline-jones-20171108-story.html

Johnson Lewis, J. (2019, February 27). *Lucy Parsons: Radical and Anarchist, Person of Color, IWW Founder.* Thought Co. https://www.thoughtco.com/lucy-parsons-biography-3530417

Johnson, S. (2018, June 26). *Sarah Chapman, Matchgirl Strike Leader.* Spitalfields Life. https://spitalfieldslife.com/2018/06/26/sarah-chapman-matchgirl-strike-leader/

Jordan, M. (2004b 1st ed.). *African -American Servitude and Historical Imaginings: Retrospective Fiction and Representation.* Palgrave Macmillian

Kanzler, K. (2005). Texts, Commodities, and Genteel Factory Girls: The Textile Mill as a Feminine Space in Antebellum American Literature. *Amerikastudien / American Studies, 50*(4), 555–573. https://www.jstor.org/stable/41158181

Karomo, C. (2022, November 7). *Sarah Chapman's story — Her inspiring tale.* Okay Bliss. https://www.okaybliss.com/sarah-chapmans-story/

Karpazli, E. (2021, October 31). *Debt we owe to working-class girls who walked out of work 133 years ago.* My London. https://www.mylondon.news/news/nostalgia/were-indebted-army-working-class-21946579

Kelly, K. (2022b). *Fight Like Hell: The History of American Labor.* Atria/One Signal Publishers.

Kelly, K. (2022, April 17). *How Black washerwomen in the South became pioneers of American labor.* Washington Post. https://www.washingtonpost.com/history/2022/04/17/black-washerwomen-strike/

Kettle, E. (2022, July 5). *Match Girls' Strike of 1888 commemorated with blue plaque in East London.* East London and West Essex Guardian Series. https://www.guardian-series.co.uk/news/20256041.match-girls-strike-1888-granted-blue-plaque-east-london/

Khan Academy. (n.d.). *Women's Labor.* Khan Academy. Retrieved March 29, 2023, from https://www.khanacademy.org/humanities/us-history/the-early-republic/culture-and-reform/a/women-in-the-workplace-and-household

Kosak, H. (1999, December 31). *Triangle Shirtwaist Fire.* Jewish Women's Archive. https://jwa.org/encyclopedia/article/triangle-shirtwaist-fire

Kühl, S. (2016). *The Angel in the House and Fallen Women: Assigning Women their Places in Victorian Society.* https://open.conted.ox.ac.uk/sites/open.conted.ox.ac.uk/files/resources/

La Neve Defrancesco, J. (2018, June 6). *Pawtucket, America's First Factory Strike.* Jacobin. https://jacobin.com/2018/06/factory-workers-strike-textile-mill-women

Library Company. (n.d.). *Harriet Farley (1817 – 1907).* Library Company. Retrieved March 29, 2023, from https://librarycompany.org/women/portraits/farley.htm

Lighter, F. (2013, July 8). *The Matchgirls strike: from a spark to a blaze.* Socialist Appeal. https://socialist.net/matchgirls-strike-125-years-on/

Lumpkin, B. (2021, August 9). *Black women laundry workers finally get their due as organizers and leaders.* People's World. https://www.peoplesworld.org/article/black-women-laundry-workers-finally-get-their-due-as-organizers-and-leaders/

Matchgirls' Memorial. (n.d.). *Fights.* Matchgirls Memorial. Retrieved April 3, 2023, from https://www.matchgirls1888.org/fights

McArthur, J. N., & Jones, J. (2019). Review of Goddess of Anarchy: The Life and Times of Lucy Parsons, American Radical. *The Southwestern Historical Quarterly, 122*(3), 356–358. https://www.jstor.org/stable/26633933

McEvoy, A. F. (1995). The Triangle Shirtwaist Factory Fire of 1911: Social Change, Industrial Accidents, and the Evolution of Common-Sense Causality. *Law & Social Inquiry, 20*(2), 621–651. https://www.jstor.org/stable/828955

Meek, C., & Nunez-Eddy, C. (2017, October 5). *The Fruits of Philosophy (1832), by Charles Knowlton.* The Embryo Project Encyclopedia. https://embryo.asu.edu/pages/fruits-philosophy-1832-charles-knowlton

Mernick. (n.d.). *The Link (1888).* Mernick. http://www.mernick.org.uk/thhol/thelink.html

Miari, A. (2018, February 22). *Annie Besant Match Girl Riots of Bow.* Roman Road London.
https://romanroadlondon.com/annie-besant-match-girl-riots-bow/

Michels, T. (1999, December 31). *Uprising of 20,000 (1909).* Jewish Women's Archive.
https://jwa.org/encyclopedia/article/uprising-of-20000-1909

Mill Girls Musical. (n.d.). *Mill Girls: A New Musical.* Mill Girls Musical. Retrieved April 27, 2023, from https://millgirlsmusical.com/

Montrie, C. (2004). "I Think Less of the Factory than of My Native Dell": Labor, Nature, and the Lowell "Mill Girls." *Environmental History, 9*(2), 275. https://doi.org/10.2307/3986087

Moran, W. (2004b) *The Belles of New England: The Women of the Textile Mills and the Families Whose Wealth They Wove* St Martin's Griffin

Murray, J. H. (1985). Class vs. Gender Identification in the "Englishwoman's Review" of the 1880s. *Victorian Periodicals Review, 18*(4), 138–142. https://www.jstor.org/stable/20082172

National Park Service. (2021, April 27). *Sarah Bagley - Lowell National Historical Park*. National Park Service. https://www.nps.gov/lowe/learn/historyculture/sarah-bagley.htm

Nettles, A. (2020, December 16). *The Radical Existence Of Lucy Parsons, The "Goddess of Anarchy."* Department of African American Studies. https://aas.princeton.edu/news/radical-existence-lucy-parsons-goddess-anarchy

New York Survey Associates, Charity Organization Society of the City of New York, & Robarts - University of Toronto. (2007). The Survey. In *Internet Archive*. East Stroudsburg, PA., Survey Associates. https://archive.org/details/thesurvey26survuoft/page/84/mode/2up (Original work published 1911)

Orleck, A. (1995). *Common sense & a little fire: women and working-class politics in the United States, 1900-1965.* The University of North Carolina Press.

Orleck, A. (1999a, December 31). *Clara Lemlich Shavelson*. Jewish Women's Archive. https://jwa.org/encyclopedia/article/shavelson-clara-lemlich

Orleck, A. (1999b, December 31). *Rose Schneiderman*. Jewish Women's Archive. https://jwa.org/encyclopedia/article/schneiderman-rose

Pankhurst, E. (1914). *My Own Story*. E. Nash.

Patmore C. (1887). *The Angel in the House.* Cassell and Co.

PBS American Experience. (n.d.). *Clara Lemlich and the Uprising of the 20,000.* PBS. https://www.pbs.org/wgbh/americanexperience/features/biography-clara-lemlich/

People's History Museum. (2020, July 5). *The Match Girls' Strike.* People's History Museum. https://phm.org.uk/blogposts/the-match-girls-strike/

Porter, L. (2020, June 18). *London History: The East End Match Girls' Strike of 1888*. Londontopia.
https://londontopia.net/columns/lauras-london/london-history-the-east-end-match-girls-strike-of-1888/

Potts, T. (2019, March 10). *Striking a Light by Louise Raw shines new light on Matchgirl strikes*. Roman Road London.
https://romanroadlondon.com/striking-a-light-louise-raw-book-review/

Raw, L. (2011). *Striking a Light* (1st ed.). Bloomsbury Publishing.

Rosen, B. (2014, April 25). *Victorian History: Bryant, May and the Match Girls*. Victorian History. http://vichist.blogspot.com/2014/04/bryant-may-and-match-girls.html

Satre, L. J. (1982). After the Match Girls' Strike: Bryant and May in the 1890s. *Victorian Studies, 26*(1), 7–31. https://www.jstor.org/stable/3827491

Schofield, A. (2018). The Uprising of the 20,000: The Making of a Labor Legend. In *A Needle, a Bobbin, a Strike: Women Needleworkers in America* (pp. 167–182). Temple University Press. https://doi.org/10.2307/j.ctv941x68.12

Schouler, W. (1845, March). *Massachusetts Lawmakers Investigate Working Conditions in Lowell: Massachusetts House Document No. 50*. Teaching American History. https://teachingamericanhistory.org/document/massachusetts-lawmakers-investigate-working-conditions-in-lowell/

Sherwood, H. (2022, February 17). *Blue plaque to honour 1888 strike by 1,400 East End matchgirls*.
The Guardian. https://www.theguardian.com/culture/2022/feb/17/blue-plaque-to-honour-1888-strike-by-1400-east-end-matchgirls

Simkin, J. (1997, September). *The 1888 London Matchgirls Strike*. Spartacus Educational. https://spartacus-educational.com/TUmatchgirls.htm

Social History for Every Classroom. (n.d.). *African-American Laundry Women Go on Strike in Atlanta.* Social History for Every Classroom. Retrieved March 29, 2023, from https://shec.ashp.cuny.edu/items/show/897

Sonnenschein, M. (2021, August 26). *Rose Schneiderman: A Woman of Valor.* Museum of Jewish Heritage — a Living Memorial to the Holocaust.

Snell, H. (1936). *Men, Movements, and Myself.* J.M. Dent and Sons, Ltd.

St. Julien, J. (2020, February, 21). *The Atlanta Washerwomen Strike of 1881.* New America. https://www.newamerica.org/better-life-lab/blog/atlanta-washerwoman-strike-1881/

Stephenson, J. (1975). Girls' Higher Education in Germany in the 1930s. *Journal of Contemporary History, 10*(1), 41–69. https://www.jstor.org/stable/260137?read-now=1&seq=2#page_scan_tab_contents

Stevenson, L. L., & Bushman, C. L. (1982). "A Good Poor Man's Wife": Being a Chronicle of Harriet Hanson Robinson and Her Family in Nineteenth-Century New England. *The New England Quarterly, 55*(2), 306. https://doi.org/10.2307/365369

Stuff You Should Know. (2022). *Short Stuff: The Atlanta Washer Woman Strike.* [YouTube video]. https://www.youtube.com/watch?v=M9SwfkVzsYc&ab_channel=StuffYouShouldKnow

The American Yawp Reader. (n.d.-a). *Harriet H. Robinson Remembers a Mill Workers' Strike, 1836.* The American Yawp Reader. Retrieved March 29, 2023, from https://www.americanyawp.com/reader/the-market-revolution/harriet-h-robinson-describes-a-mill-workers-strike-1863/

The American Yawp Reader. (n.d.-b). *Lucy Parsons on Women and Revolutionary Socialism (1905).* The American Yawp Reader. Retrieved March 29, 2023, from https://www.americanyawp.com/reader/16-capital-and-labor/lucy-parsons-on-women-and-revolutionary-socialism-1905/

The Attic. (n.d.). *The Myth of the Mill Girls*. The Attic. Retrieved March 29, 2023, from https://www.theattic.space/home-page-blogs/2018/8/30/the-myth-of-the-mill-girls

The Matchgirls Memorial. (n.d.). *The Story of the Strike*. Matchgirls Memorial. Retrieved March 29, 2023, from https://www.matchgirls1888.org/the-story-of-the-strike

The Voice of Industry. (1845, January 15). *Petition and Legislature*. Industrial Revolution. https://www.industrialrevolution.org/petition-and-legislature.html

Tilly, L. A. (1994). Women, Women's History, and the Industrial Revolution. *Social Research, 61*(1), 115–137. https://www.jstor.org/stable/40971024

TUC150. (2018, July 16). *Match Women's Strike*. TUC 150 Stories. https://tuc150.tuc.org.uk/stories/match-womens-strike/

Tyrrell, C. (n.d.). *Sarah George Bagley*.

Sutori. Retrieved March 29, 2023, from https://www.sutori.com/en/story/sarah-george-bagley--HdWGkbuKWarvjNawtDSRsx5s

Unison. (2021, March 8). *Remembering the matchgirls who struck for better pay and conditions*. Unison. https://www.unison.org.uk/news/article/2021/03/remembering-matchgirls-struck-better-pay-conditions/

University of Albany. (n.d.). *Mary Paul Letters*. University of Albany. Retrieved March 29, 2023, from https://www.albany.edu/history/history316/MaryPaulLetters.html

University of Toronto Library. (1911, April 8). *The Survey*. Internet Archive. https://archive.org/stream/thesurvey26survuoft/thesurvey26survuoft_djvu.txt

Unladylike 2020. (n.d.). *Rose Schneiderman*. Unladylike 2020. Retrieved March 29, 2023, from https://unladylike2020.com/profile/rose-schneiderman/

Wang, J. (2002). Gender, Race and Civilization: The Competition between American Power Laundries and Chinese Steam Laundries, 1870s - 1920s. *American Studies International, 40*(1), 52–73.
https://www.jstor.org/stable/41280954

Wang, J. S. (2004). Race, Gender, and Laundry Work: The Roles of Chinese Laundrymen and American Women in the United States, 1850-1950.
Journal of American Ethnic History, 24(1), 58–99. https://www.jstor.org/stable/27501531

Warren, E. (2019, November 21). *Elizabeth's Prepared Remarks at Clark Atlanta University*. Elizabeth Warren.

Williams, M. (1892). *Round London, Down East and Up West*. Macmillan & Co.

Wright, H. (1979). Sarah G. Bagley. *Labor History, 20*(3), 398.

www.ingramcontent.com/pod-product-compliance
Lightning Source LLC
Chambersburg PA
CBHW031116080526
44587CB00011B/994